SO, YOU'RE TRANSGENDER. NOW WHAT?

The Guide for Transgender People and Their Loved Ones.

Stephania M. Kanitsch

"Coming out pretty much meant I needed to be okay with dying. So, it became a question of facing death but feeling alive or being a walking zombie that was dead inside."
—Anonymous

I dedicate this book to my loving wife, Sharon Kanitsch who has stuck by me through all the difficulties of my transition. I love you. I also dedicate it to my counselor, Cari Foote, MA, LPC-S, LMFT-S. Cari has guided me through the darkness of my depression and the newness in my life. Her suggestions and counseling help me daily. Much appreciation and thanks go to her. I also dedicate this work to all transgender individuals who have discovered themselves, those just discovering themselves, and those that are uncertain. I desire for forthcoming generations that transgender individuals are just treated as humans as they should be.

Stephania M. Kanitsch

Cover designed by Jennifer Alt

This book supplies insight into the transgender phenomenon. Within this book, the reader will find information on transitioning, provide loved ones with a view of the transgender life. The ups, downs, happiness, and sadness of being transgender.

Stephania M. Kanitsch
Visit my website at www.SpanningGenderBooks.com

Printed in the United States of America

First Printing: April 2019
Amazon.com

TABLE OF CONTENTS

INTRODUCTION

I authored this book for the reader to understand what they are walking into once they know they are transgender. It provides insight into the process of discovery as well. Some information I provide may not be found in other books of the same topic. These include the cycle of oppression, discrimination and its effects, bathroom bills, and others.

This helps the reader to understand the highs of being transgender and transitioning. It also provides information on some of the more negative sides of being transgender. In no way am I trying to scare a person from transitioning. Quite the opposite. I am providing this added information, so the reader is ready for the negative things that may happen.

I hope that anyone grasping they are transgender would transition. I went through 55 years of pretending to be a male. It freed me from those shackles when I came out in 2013. Even though my clinical depression is still bad, I now live my life as the true me. I can look in a mirror and see her. Most people do not achieve authenticity in their life. They may have a fear of being different. It can make for a hard life. Be authentic, be proud, be you.

The first section is about defining gender and provides a history of special transgender days and some gender definitions. You will also find definitions in the preface and Appendix One. The acronyms used in this book are in Appendix One.

The second section is figuring out if you are transgender. There are suggestions to help you come to your conclusion. Why it may confuse you and provides explanations for some of the identities outside the norm.

The third section is about your transgender or gender-expansive child and how you should handle your surprise announcement from your child. This section also provides information on what might happen if you restrict your child from being able to express their gender. It is a must read for any parent going through this with their child.

Section four provides information to help you in your decision on transitioning.

Section five is about religion. I added this section because many transgender individuals are spiritual or religious. Here I provide a list of major religions and their acceptance or nonacceptance of transgender parishioners. I hope that this section will save the reader from the heartache I faced when I went back to church.

Section six is on transitioning. It provides chapters on the diverse types or steps of your transition. This section also provides the different requirements for both medical and surgeries available that you may want. If you transition, this section will provide help in the different steps.

The seventh section is about discrimination, oppression, prejudice, among other negative parts of being transgender. I provide insight into the cycle of oppression and just why it is a cycle.

Section eight is about suicide in the transgender community and why it is at epidemic levels. Over 40 percent of transgender adults have attempted suicide in their life. There are many reasons for this. I go into some of these reasons along with why the use of mental health treatment is so high in the transgender community.

Section nine provides a little insight on how to care for your transgender loved one.

Section ten provides information that did not fit under any other topic, but I felt was important.

I would love to hear from my readers on any other topics they may want to see in a future book on being transgender. Thanks for selecting my book as a resource. Happy reading.

PREFACE

I penned this publication because coming out and being out as transgender can be a daunting journey. I want to give the transgender person and their loved ones the information and facts to navigate being transgender. Information is power. Use this power to ensure a smooth transition and a loving life. Being transgender is more than transitioning. It is the ability of the transgender person to spot the completeness most cisgender people take for granted or never understand. (cisgender people are those whose gender and assigned sex at birth match) There is a reference section at the back of this work for further support.

I have included negative topics in this book. It is best to have that knowledge. Though I included these topics in this work, do not let it stop or scare you from being who you are. Quite the opposite, I want to provide you with the means to be yourself. I want this book to supply the facts, so you have knowledge of the possibilities of negative responses. I authored this book to allow you to have the insight to ensure your journey is as positive as possible. You will endure loses and hurt associated with your transition. Make sure the positives shine brighter.

When I came out, the information and support available were limited in my locale. I got support through online support groups but most of my support came from reading. I need to understand everything I undertake. My research into being transgender was extensive. I want to use this knowledge to help others.

I spent time on a board of directors for a nonprofit and served as their vice president. During my tenure, I wrote seminars providing insight into the whole LGBTQ community. One seminar was specific to the transgender community. I grasped then I could supply information valuable to this community. Loved ones also prodded me to write books after my exit from the nonprofit.

I put my heart and soul into those seminars. You will find throughout this book my passion for the transgender community. The same passion I put into the seminars is in this book.

The more we educate the public, the easier it will be for the transgender individual to exist in society. This makes life fuller for the transgender community.

I hope within the time I have left in this life we will see change. The suicide rate for all people rises every year. There has been an increase in hate. How can you hate someone you do not know? Because of what they wear, how they look, or how they identify? If this book saves one person, it was worth every second I put into it. If it saves more, even better.

I hope this book opens hearts and minds showing transgender people are human beings, like everyone else. We work, play, and love like everyone else. We are family, friends, coworkers, and everyday people.

This book uses transgender as a way of inclusivity for the whole gender non-conforming community.

Some topics may seem like they do not fit, but I include them for reference and information.

There is something near to my heart. It is the high death rate in the transgender community. Whether by suicide, health, or homicide, it is devastating for the transgender community. I supply the Trans Lifeline numbers for reference throughout this book. I want the transgender person to remember there is someone there to talk to. Reach out to someone, anyone. Do not take your life. It is valuable. We love you.

Life gets better. Bad things do not last. Things get better. Life will get better. Reach out, please. For me.

Trans Lifeline: US: 877-565-8860 Canada: 877-330-6366

Words used throughout the book.

Sex:—Either of the two main categories (male and female) in which we divide humans based on sex characteristics. Also see: sex assigned at birth.

Gender:—Gender is who you know you are in your brain. They used to use a person's sex characteristics to determine gender. They now find it is how a person knows and not tied to a person's sex. There are people will not accept this.

Cisgender:—A person whose sense of gender corresponds to their birth sex. A cisgender person is not transgender. Cisgender is not a slur. It differentiates between gender variant and non-gender variant people. Cisgendered and cisgenders are not words.

Gender Expression:—How a person expresses their gender identity is through their appearance, dress, and behavior. It does not equal gender. It is when you express the gender you know you are or feel. Most transgender people use gender expression to match their gender identity. Someone with a non-conforming gender expression may or may not be transgender.

Gender Identity:—A person's internal sense of self. Everyone has a gender identity. A transgender person's sex assigned at birth and their gender identity is not the same.

Sex Assigned at Birth (SAAB) :—The biological sex a doctor assigns a person at birth. This is not their gender. The doctor assigns sex by physical anatomy at birth, and/or karyotyping.

Transgender/Trans:—Umbrella term for those whose gender identity differs from the sex assigned at birth. Transgendered or transgenders is not a word.

Transition:—Going from your birth gender to your known gender by using gender expression. Changing from one gender to another. Social transition is the least most transgender people do.

Transsexual:—Transsexual predates the use of transgender for identifying transgender people. Some identify as transsexual if they are going through medical or surgical procedures. Unlike transgender/trans, transsexual is not an umbrella term. Some transgender people consider transsexual derogatory. It is best to not use this term to identify a person as transsexual unless they have asked you to.

PART ONE

Definition of Transgender

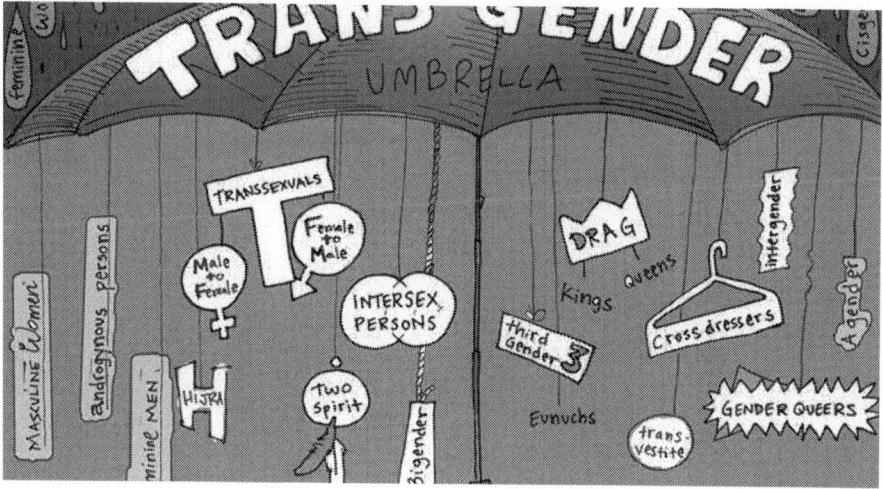

CHAPTER ONE: TRANSGENDER – THE BASICS

"What matters most is not 'what' you are,
but 'who' you are."
—DaShanne Stokes

Most people walk around every day happily in the body they are born in. A small group recognizes their bodies do not fit their perception of who they are. In a world where there are unwritten societal standards, it makes it hard for this small group to exist. The transgender community is a special community. Though they experience oppression, they move forward to be their authentic selves. People do not understand what being transgender is. Transgender people also may not understand it at first. This misunderstanding partially comes from the portrayal of the transgender community through media. Stereotypes about transgender people enhance this. A lack of knowledge of what transgender is also can skew people's opinions. When we are out in public, we can educate those we meet and allow them to see we are regular humans.

Media portrays the transgender community as drag kings, drag queens, transvestites, and cross-dressers. Some believe gender and sex characteristics are the same things. They also believe gender is a part of a person's DNA. This is false.

Females have XX chromosomes and males XY. Wait! A person's chromosomes determine the sex of the person, not gender. But chromosomes do not always determine sex. There are variations in chromosomes where females have XY chromosomes and males have XX chromosomes. People may have only one X or one Y chromosome. Sometimes, there may be 3 letters together such as XXX, XYY, or XXY. There are other chromosome combinations humans have. Thus, chromosomes do not always determine sex.

Another argument is women have women parts and men have men parts. Ask yourself what is your definition of women and men? It is not an easy question to answer. Dependent on your answer you will always leave someone out. Any definition leaving someone out is not a valid definition.

To define a man or woman is not as easy as you may think. This does not mean one day they are male and the next day they are female. When they come out as transgender and start their transition, they commit to who they are. For many, part of their commitment is to start hormones or changing their name.

We are talking about gender, transgender to be exact. Gender is the internal sense or knowledge of who you are as a person. For a transgender person, this sense of self does not match their primary sex characteristics. For many transgender people, this perception may onset as early as 2 or 3 years old. Discerning the difference may not be clear, but they know something is different. This is scary.

At 3 or 4 years old I knew I was different. This included wanting to play with the other gender's toys and not the gender assigned at birth. I wanted to play house and play with dolls. Living in the 1960s and 1970s was a different time for being transgender (transsexual then).

At that time in transgender history, many who were transgender went to Trinidad, Colorado to transition. Trinidad was the only place in the United States performing surgeries for the transgender individual back then. After their transition, the transgender person would start a new life with their new name and gender.

Transgender people may experience gender dysphoria. Gender dysphoria manifests because of the incongruence of their body and mind. This can cause depression, anxiety, and stress. It can manifest to the point of suicidal thoughts or worse. When older transgender people transition later in life, I believe it is because their gender dysphoria manifests. There are other reasons. When a transgender person looks in a mirror, they do not see the person they know to be true in their heart and brain. We will talk about gender dysphoria later in the book.

The transgender community comprises many smaller communities. They are gender fluid, non-binary, agender, and others. People who fall under the transgender continuum may not identify as transgender. Many people see gender as either/or (male/female). Gender exists on a continuum from the masculine to the feminine.

Gender fluid people may not identify as male or female. Their gender expression may be male for a while, then female for a while. Gender fluid people may also express as a mix. They might sport a beard while dressing feminine.

Gender-expansive is anyone identifying outside society's norms. It covers transgender and non-binary identities. People are using gender-expansive more because it better identifies those not binary.

Even though I do not believe in the gender binary, we will use it in this book. This makes it easier to explain the differences.

The transgender community is small but diverse. (0.6 percent, or 1.4 million people in the U.S.) Transgender people are many cultures, religions, ethnicities, and other differing qualities.

A transgender person lacks no abilities cisgender people have. Being transgender is not a mental health illness. Many transgender people have mental health problems caused by daily oppression.

CHAPTER TWO: WHAT TRANSGENDER IS AND IS NOT

"It's not my appearance that defines me.
It's my heart and soul."
—Anonymous

The definition of transgender is vague. So, who is under the transgender umbrella? It is anyone expressing gender outside their assigned sex at birth (ASAB). For some who are on the gender spectrum, they may not like the label's society applies to them. Why can't we be human beings with different expressions of who we are without labels?

There are those in society who may look at us as cross-dressers. Some transgender people dress as the other gender prior to coming out and transitioning. This in no way makes them a cross-dresser. They may be transgender expressing themselves as their identity but may not be out as transgender yet.

Note: Cross-dressers are people who sometimes wear clothes associated with the opposite sex for self-expression. They are a heterosexual (= not gay) man.

Drag kings and queens are entertainers. Drag kings and queens may come out as transgender. On Ru Paul's Drag Race there have been a few drag queens who have come out as transgender, including Ru Paul.

Society sees gender as either/or and looks down on anyone outside the gender binary. (gender binary = male/female.) This book will review recent research on what makes people transgender. This research confirms what transgender people already know. We were born this way. It is not because of trauma or other bad experiences. The environment can influence gender and affectional orientation, but the influence is slight.

In the past, transsexual was the term to signify a transgender person. Transsexual currently identifies a person who is going through their medical and/or surgical transition. Some people in the transgender community view the word as derogatory. This may be because there are slang words which developed from transsexual which signify transgender people in the sex industry.

CHAPTER THREE: WHY GENDER IS NOT BINARY

People assume gender is a strict progression of male-to-female. But actually, it's more like a big ball of wibbly-wobbly gendery-bendery stuff.
—Anonymous

Many in society believe there are only the binary genders (male/female). We receive these gender binary signals from an early age. When we are born the doctor claims, we are a boy or girl. When a hospital discharges a baby, they release them in blue blankets for males and pink for females. Labels given to babies in the hospital does not equate back to their gender. How a child feels inside determines their gender.

Humans have the gender binary ingrained into our brains from an early age. Here is a list of ways society promotes the gender binary from an early age:

•—Supposed to fit gender roles set by parents.
•—TV, movies and other media push compliance with certain gender roles.
•—Most schools require children to play with boys if they were born male or girls if they were born female.
•—Parents tell them if their sex at birth is male to act a certain way, and if their sex at birth is female to act a certain way.
•—Religious beliefs of their parents.
•—Rewarded for acting the correct "gender."
•—Scolded or worse for acting the wrong "gender."
•—If they feel uncomfortable expressing who they are.
•—No one else talks about a sense of self this way, thus thinking they are the only one with these feelings.
•—They try to act as their AGAB (assumed gender at birth).
•—Shame, embarrassment, and guilt for expressing who they are. <1>

Many children play with both genders' toys. (Note: I do not believe in gendering any toy or garment.) The same goes for clothes, hair, and other ways to express gender.

It is important for humans to express their true self. Society looks down on those who do not follow society's norms. Society puts people into boxes expecting everyone to follow society's beliefs. The human brain does not work within a limited space. Everyone is different and should express who they know they are. When transgender individuals come out, most bust the label box apart to never live by confining labels again.

Non-binary people are why the gender binary does not actually exist. There are people who may dress up wearing a dress and have a mustache and beard. Why do people consider this strange? They are expressing who they are and how they acknowledge their feeling of self.

Research shows 12 percent of the Millennial Generation identify as gender non-conforming or transgender. <2> Younger generations accept people for who they are. (most do) Gender queer is not a set gender. It is when a person expresses who they are daily. This could be male one day, female the next day, and androgynous the next day.

I want to see a world where a person can be themselves without being oppressed. Even though society is heading this way, it is my belief I will not see this become a reality in my life. I hope this book and the future of humankind will get to where people can express themselves without reprisal.

<1>—Dara Hoffman-Fox, L. (2017). You and Your Gender Identity, A Guide to Discovery. New York City: Skyhorse Publishing.
<2>—GLAAD, March 30, 2017, New GLAAD study reveals twenty percent of millennials identify as LGBTQ, https://www.glaad.org/blog/new-glaad-study-reveals-twenty-percent-millennials-identify-lgbtq

CHAPTER FOUR: TRANSGENDER PIONEERS IN THE UNITED STATES

"I believe much more in love and heart. That's much bigger [than] to see what you have in the middle of your legs."
—Lea T

Many transgender people are pioneers. It is important to know where we used to be, so we can move forward. We will also look at the history of GCS (gender confirmation surgery). These GCS pioneers are a part of how the transgender community has gotten to where we are today.

Below is a list of the pioneers who shaped the transgender community over time:

* - 1952—Christine Jorgensen is the first American receiving GCS that became public. Her surgery made her known as the first transsexual in the media. She brought awareness of transgender issues.
* - 1966—In San Francisco, the Compton Cafeteria riots took place. Transgender women took a stand there against discrimination and police harassment.
* - 1966—Dr. Harry Benjamin published "The Transgender Phenomenon". This later became the WPATH Standards of Care.
* - 1969—Transgender people were at the forefront of starting the Stonewall Riots in New York City. This sparked the U.S. gay rights movement.
* - 1977—Renee Richards won a Supreme Court ruling to play professional tennis as a transgender woman.
* - 1979—WPATH (World Professional Association of Transgender Health) releases the first version of the Standards of Care. Version 8 should publish in 2019. "The Transsexual Phenomenon" was a forerunner to the WPATH Standards of Care. WPATH is an international association to formalize health care for the transgender community.
* - 1986 An advocacy group, FTM International launches. Founded by Lou Sullivan it challenged claims transgender men are not gay. He died in 1991 from AIDS.
* - 1989—Upon his death in Spokane, Washington Jazz musician Billy Tipton had female sex characteristics. Billy lived for 56 years as a man, marrying several times, and raising children.
* - 1993—Brandon Teena, a transgender male is murdered in Nebraska. The movie "Boys Don't Cry" documented his story to a national audience.

* – 1993—Cheryl Chase founded the Intersex Society of North America (ISNA). This organization helps build awareness of the intersex community.
* – 1998—Rita Hester is murdered in Massachusetts. Her death inspired the Transgender Day of Remembrance (TDOR).
* – 1999—The first ever International Transgender Day of Observance. This commemorates the deaths of transgender people. The transgender community observes this yearly on November 20. <1>
* – 2002—The Transgender Law Center is started. The law center advocates to change laws, policies, and attitudes to ensure equal rights, no matter their identity.
* – 2003—National Center for Transgender Equality (NCTE) is founded. NCTE fights to advance equality by supplying advocacy, collaboration, and empowerment.
* – 2009—Chaz Bono, the child of Sonny and Cher comes out as transgender and starts his transition.
* – 2009—President Barack Obama signs a federal hate crimes law. This law covers crimes motivated by bias to marginalized communities.
* – 2010—Amanda Simpson becomes the first transgender presidential appointee. They appointed her senior technical advisor in the Commerce Department.
* – 2010—Players of the Ladies Professional Golf Association vote to allow transgender women to compete.
* – 2011—Janet Mock, a People.com editor and author in 2011, comes out as transgender.
* – 2012—Miss Universe allowed transgender women to compete.
* – 2013—The American Psychiatric Association (APA) updates its diagnostic manual, removing gender identity disorder. Gender dysphoria becomes a disorder brought on by being transgender.
* – 2014—Actress Laverne Cox becomes the first transgender person featured on the cover of Time magazine.
* – 2015—Caitlyn Jenner completes her gender transition and appears on the cover of Vanity Fair.
* – 2016—The U.S. military lifts its ban on transgender service members. The Obama administration recommends public schools allow transgender students to use restrooms and locker rooms matching the gender they identify as.
* – 2017—The Trump administration revokes the Obama-era directive, saying we should set policies for transgender students' bathroom access at the state and local levels. <2>

<1> trans_timeline.pdf. (n.d.). Retrieved from UC Riverside: https://www.ucr.edu/search-results?q=trans%20timeline&search-by=all

<2> key-dates-for-transgender-rights-in-the-us. (n.d.). Retrieved from Seattle Times: https://www.seattletimes.com/nation-world/key-dates-for-transgender-rights-in-the-us/

CHAPTER FIVE: SPECIAL DAYS IN THE TRANSGENDER COMMUNITY

People will stare. Make it worth their while.
—Harry Winston

The transgender community has special days, weeks, and months set aside to celebrate and remember those who have gone before us.

Below is a list of those special days and what makes them special:

* - April 1996—Day of Silence. First celebrated in 1996. The day in April varies from year to year.
* - May 17—International Day Against Homophobia, Transphobia, and Biphobia. First celebrated in 2005. This day shows awareness of violence, discrimination, and repression of LGBTQ communities worldwide.
* - March 31—International Transgender Day of Visibility. First celebrated in 2009, it is for bringing awareness to transgender people and their identities. It also recognizes the advocates fighting for transgender rights.
* - October—LGBTQ History Month. First celebrated in 1994. Set aside to encourage remembering LGBTQ history.
* - June—LGBTQ Pride Month. This is the month the LGBTQ community celebrates its adversity. The Stonewall Riots happened in June. Legalization of same-sex marriage in the United States became a reality in June 2015. Many cities have their pride celebrations in June, but many pride events go on all year long. The Pulse Nightclub massacre also happened in June, making it a somber time.
* - October 11—National Coming Out Day. First celebrated in 1988, this day celebrates coming out. It is also a time for those already out to reflect on their lives as their authentic selves.
* - First Sunday of November—Transgender Parents Day—First celebrated in 2009. A day honoring transgender parents, and parents of transgender children.
* - November—Transgender Awareness Month. November is for the public to realize the transgender community. It portrays the struggles transgender people face in everyday life. It is also a time to reflect on the violence and losses of the transgender community faces.
* - November 14th to November 20th. Transgender Awareness Week. This week allows the community to help others recognize the transgender community. The Transgender Awareness Week ends on the Transgender Day of Remembrance (TDOR).

* - November 20—Transgender Day of Remembrance. The first year of TDOR was in 1999. We remember the transgender people who lost their lives to violence on this day.

PART TWO

How Do I Know I'm Transgender?

CHAPTER ONE: THE REALITY OF GENDER

"I didn't realize who I was until I stopped
being who I wasn't."
—The Minds Journal

B road knowledge comes from a great education. If you think you may be transgender, the best thing to do is educate yourself on what transgender is. So how do you know? Confusion in these feelings does not help. This chapter will cover how you may determine this answer.

Within this section, we will go into what non-binary is and why some do not consider it to be transgender. I explain what gender non-conforming (GNC) is and is not. The gender binary is no longer alive and well. (gender binary is the belief there are only two genders, male and female) Gender exists on a continuum. I use the gender binary to supply a reference for easier understanding.

This chapter will allow you to figure where you may be on the gender spectrum. For some people, it is easy to conclude what their gender identity is. It may confuse others to come to this conclusion. They may want to experiment with what feels right for them. There is no wrong way to be you.

One thing to remember. Sex at birth does not determine gender at birth. It determines physical sex characteristics at birth. (intersex is a condition where the person may have ambiguous genitalia) No one can determine your gender except you. For most, this feeling matches your sexual characteristics.

Once reality hits you, it may be a relief. It is human nature to want to know where we fit in. This makes it easier to find people like you who will accept you with open arms. If you prefer no label, do it.

CHAPTER TWO: THE CONFUSION

"I found power in accepting the truth of who I am. It may not be a truth that others can accept, but I cannot live any other way. How would it be to live a lie every minute of your life?"
—Alison Goodman, Eon: Dragoneye Reborn

The confusion a person has with their gender identity may show their identity is gender-expansive. Relief comes when the confusion subsides.

Some transgender people may find attraction towards the opposite gender. This is not unusual. Being transgender does not imply being gay. Transgender people have different affectional orientations like cisgender people. For many transgender people, this is a reality. They may come out as gay only to find the confusion does not subside.

Transgender people, upon realization of who they are, are the gender they identify as. This means any relationship they are in changes orientation once they come out. Transgender people in a heterosexual relationship become gay. Those whose attraction was for the same-sex before coming out would be heterosexual after coming out.

This can get quite confusing itself. Remember, you are you and only you can figure it out.

You may find through this confusion it is hard to pin down your identity. Being honest of your gender you may find your affectional attraction broadens. If you remain confused, try to find a gender expression you feel comfortable with. Express as androgynous and see if it relieves your anxiety. Whatever you do, it is your life and allows you the time to reflect on your true feelings. It is OK, you can change upon your realization of your true identity. Coming out as transgender has a much higher stigma than coming out as gay. If you come out as gay first, you may find it easier when you come out as transgender.

Transgender people may experience disappointment in themselves or in how they look. Transgender people can get gender dysphoria. Gender dysphoria comes from the in-congruency transgender people feel. Gender dysphoria can become extreme to the point of trying or committing suicide. If you feel you need to take your life, please do not. Life gets better and being your true self helps. The Trans

Lifeline has telephone support for transgender people in crisis. It is for transgender people, run by transgender people. You talk only to transgender people. If you are contemplating suicide, please call them or other hotlines. Your life is important.

Trans Lifeline - US: 877-565-8860 Canada: 877-330-6366

CHAPTER THREE: SO, HOW DO I KNOW MY GENDER IDENTITY?

"Identity cannot be found or fabricated but emerges
from within when one has the courage to let go."
—Doug Cooper

How do I know I am transgender? This may be one of the hardest questions to answer. Stigmas weighing down the transgender community may also make it hard to come out. There are ways to help in your discovery. Gender therapists are available and helpful.

Talk to someone who is transgender. Ask them questions. Tell them how you feel. Find a local support group or online transgender group. Even if you can relate to someone's story, never tell them they are transgender. These resources may be some of the most valuable you can find. Let no one tell you your identity. You determine your gender.

There is no test, medical, or otherwise to show you are transgender. Websites and books may give you some insight into your gender identity. Nothing supplies absolute assurance of your gender except your own feelings.

There are apps available, and websites with tests to determine your gender. I will not say do not use it. If you do, do not let the results influence your discovery of who you are. Most of these tests have loaded questions which may push your gender the wrong way. Why are you taking the test? Because you know something is different. If your non-binary or gender fluid, these tests do not supply the correct answer. Believe in your feelings. Do not allow outside influences. Do your research.

The following are ways to help you determine your gender:

Sit down and write out what you are feeling. This may entail not liking who you are or what you see in the mirror. Maybe you dislike the pronouns used to address you. You may find an interest in clothing and commercials that relate better to your gender. Growing your hair if you determine you are a transgender female. Cutting your hair short if you are a transgender male.

It is best to understand your gender expression may not signify you are transgender. It is one sign you may be transgender or non-binary. By talking with others who feel the way you do it may give insight into what your identity is. This is your journey and your discovery, no one else's.

Ask yourself some questions about how you feel. This may direct your feelings towards your answer. If you dislike how you look in the mirror unless you express the other gender, you may be transgender. Be sure when asking yourself these questions you also put them on paper. It may be important to come back to your answers later. Remember though these are suggestions on finding the answer. This book only supplies guidance.

Ask yourself whether these feelings might be non-binary. It is best to understand you may be a feminine man or a masculine woman. Reread your answers and any other notes you have written. Rate your notes and feelings for importance. This can help guide you. Feelings felt less often may exist which you have forgotten. By reading your notes later you may find your answer.

If you are an adult, try to remember your childhood experiences. Did you prefer the opposite genders toys or clothes? Did you dress up in your mother's or sister's clothes? Did you play house? There are children who do these things because of curiosity. In no way does this mean you are transgender. Putting these feelings with other findings may signal your identity.

Do you feel alienated in society? Do you feel uncomfortable around others born the same-sex as you?

Your given name and assumed pronouns may feel like they do not fit. This may make you uncomfortable when others address you because you do not fit who you are. This may make you uncomfortable. Check for gender dysphoria. When you started puberty did the changes to your body upset you? Write your questions and your answers. The notes you keep can become valuable.

Explore online forums and websites supplying information on self-discovery. Information is power. Educating yourself by reading this book is a good start. At the back of this book is a reference section. The reference section has information which may become invaluable.

Ensure to leave all your options open. Try different identities including a binary transgender person. (Transgender male or female) If something does not feel right try somewhere else on the gender continuum. You may even want to try androgynous for a while. By doing this you may find it easier to find your identity. You need not to dress the part. Imagine your life in this new gender. Write your feelings for each different expression.

If the transgender binary does not feel comfortable you might express non-binary. By discovering yourself this way you may find you are gender fluid.

Ensure that the transgender person accomplishes self-care. This is important because being transgender can cause undue stress. Do things you enjoy. Try something new you have always wanted to do. Listening to music or walking can help reduce stress and make you feel better.

The following are questions to ask yourself to find your identity:

• – Did you have fantasies or dreams you were a gender other than the one the doctor claimed you were at birth?
• – Play with items society says your assigned gender should not play with?
• – Wishing to or dressing up for Halloween as the gender you feel you are?
• – Did you blow out the candles on a cake wishing you were a different gender?
• – Asking Santa Claus to make you the right gender?
• – Praying to God you would wake up as the correct gender?
• – Praying to God to take you to heaven so you could come back as the correct gender?
• – Did you try to be or act like the gender you were born with, hoping you might accept it?
• – Have you thought about removing offending parts from your body with knives or scissors?
• – Older people may have known their whole life but want to transition to their gender identity before they die. This is important because families may not live up to your wishes in your death.

If you are transgender, act your gender. If you are gender fluid, act it. Be your true self. Being yourself may also relieve any stress you may have. There are far too many ways to accept your gender is different.

CHAPTER FOUR: NON-BINARY (NB)

"The first thing you're going to want to know about me
is:
Am I a boy, or am I a girl?"
— Jeff Garvin, Symptoms of Being Human

Non-binary people prefer to not identify as transgender. This is because of stereotypes and stigmas against the transgender community.

Non-binary is anyone not part of the gender binary (male/female). All the gender identities beyond male or female are non-binary. This includes gender fluid, androgyne, agender, among others. (listed in references in Part Eleven)

Gender non-conforming can be any person who is not their birth gender and outside the binary. By educating society we may open their eyes to why gender is not male or female. Gender is also not a choice a person makes.

There are many activities people consider either male or female activities. Gender and societal norms make it harder for transgender people to accept themselves. Display of these norms starts at an early age and continues through life.

Because of cisnormativity, being outside the norms differentiates transgender from cis. Cisnormativity can also place more anxiety and pressure on the transgender person.

Note: Cisnormativity is the belief that most, if not all people are cisgender. This belief disqualifies transgender people by not recognizing them

NB signifies non-binary. Some non-binary people also use enbee. This may confuse you. Wait for the next sub-chapter, gender non-conforming. It is even more fun.

The pressures and nonacceptance fuel the bad mental health of transgender people.

CHAPTER FIVE: GENDER NON-CONFORMING (GNC)

Not a girl. Not a boy. Not your business.
—Anonymous

Gender non-conforming? So, what is that? Gender non-conforming is quite a few different things, and others it is not. I hope I have not confused you yet. When we first come out and learn who we are it is hard to keep track of all this. Gender non-conforming people can be transgender. That is not a rule. Gender non-conforming people can be intersex. Again, it is not a rule. Gender non-conforming can identify non-binary, transgender, intersex, or gender-expansive. That is not a rule. Gender non-conforming are those that are not transgender binary.

This may confuse you, so follow me. There are many words in the transgender community that have an ambiguous meaning. Each meaning may overlap. Some words carry a higher stigma than others.

One thing gender non-conforming is not is transgender binary gender. There are intersex people who do not identify in the transgender spectrum at all. They may not even know they are intersex. Other intersex people may identify as transgender. This is because the doctors mutilated their genitalia reconstructing it with surgery and kept the wrong genitals at birth.

Note: Intersex is a condition in which a person is born with genitalia or other reproductive parts that do not fit the typical definitions of female or male.

I hate to use this, but gender non-conforming is all gender meanings. It is also none of the meanings. What I mean is all the different genders besides binary fit as gender non-conforming. It is a better definition of genderqueer.

But genderqueer can be transgender binary. Genderqueer describes a person not living within societies gender norms. Gender variant is another phrase for gender non-conforming.

Phew! Glad we cleared that up. It is best to ask a person how they identify if they identify at all. By asking, you may save yourself or them from embarrassment.

CHAPTER SIX: INTERSEX

"our society is unequal, and bodily difference is used to justify that inequality."
—Emer O'Toole, Girls Will Be Girls: Dressing Up, Playing Parts and Daring to Act Differently Chapter

Transgender individual's issue is gender identity. Intersex people's issue is their primary sex characteristics. Intersex is a condition where a person may have ambiguous genitalia. There are other variations. Intersex is not transgender.

What happens to many intersex people at birth is what may make them transgender. Because of their ambiguous genitalia, intersex babies are "corrected." This correction is mutilation of their genitals to make them male or female. There are other things that may cause them being transgender. As with other identities they are not transgender because they are intersex. They may be transgender because the genital the doctor left at birth was not the correct one.

Intersex describes variations in chromosomes, genitalia, and reproductive anatomy at birth. Intersex is when a person is born with an anatomy that someone decided is neither male or female. The Intersex Society of North America (ISNA) adopted the term Disorders of Sex Development (DSD) in 2006.

They used to recognize intersex people as hermaphrodites. Some still refer to them as hermaphrodites, but it is a derogatory word. The most common variations are when an intersex person is born with genitalia of both sexes. There are many other variations I will not get into. Check the ISNA website for more information. http://www.isna.org/

Some doctors' "correct" genitalia to the recognizable sex of the infant if they are ambiguous. This practice needs to end and allow the child, when mature enough, to make this decision. This puts undue stress on them if they then identify as transgender. By mutilating them they may not get GCS because of the mutilation. Many consider themselves transgender. If doctors' and parents stop mutilating the infant, it may lower the number of intersex people identifying as transgender.

CHAPTER SEVEN: COMING OUT

"I don't know how people do this. How Blue did this.
Two words. Two freaking words, and I'm not the same
Simon anymore."
—Becky Albertalli, Simon vs. the Homo Sapiens Agenda

Coming out as transgender can invigorate and scare at the same time. It can unshackle you to be authentic. You may find it harder if you already know how family and friends feel about LGBTQ people. Everyone is different. There is no one right way to come out.

Come out to yourself before coming out to anyone else. Know who you are as a person. If you feel you are transgender binary, make sure you are. If you are non-binary, ensure yourself you are. This makes it easier for you to explain when you come out.

Coming out is a personal decision and different for each person. Remember that coming out as transgender differs from coming out as LGB. People know what it means to be gay, lesbian, or bisexual. Most people do not know what being transgender is.

Your timing of coming out is also your decision. Let no one force you. If you come out before starting your transition, this is all right. Others may want to wait until they have been on hormones long enough for some of the changes to start. These decisions are yours to make. The decision process should take into consideration your living situation and safety.

There is one question many transgender people ask. Why do transgender people have to come out as transgender, but cisgender people do not have to come out as cis? (cisgender) This is the transgender person's chance to announce what pronouns they want to use. If they have had forward thought, they may already have a name to let people know. If your gender is outside the binary, let them know what your gender identity is. You may also want to explain what your identity entails.

Coming out is difficult for anyone whether transgender or another LGBTQ identity. This is the same for any LGBTQ person. What happens after coming out is different.

Some transgender people may know who they are but do not transition until they feel safe and comfortable enough to come out. This is smart advice if you can take the gender dysphoria for longer. If you lose family and friends make sure you have other living arrangements, so you are not out on the streets.

There are as many ways to come out as there are people. Some LGBTQ people put a lot of thought into their coming out. Remember, this is your time. Enjoy it. Do not let those you come out to destroy this time.

Some of the more common ways of coming out are by letter, email, face to face, video, or social media.

I came out to my wife and counselor face to face. I was ready to lose my marriage and my house because I knew I had to do this. For family and friends, I waited five months until my breast growth showed. I wanted to ensure this was my identity.

My preferred way was sending emails and PM's through Facebook to my family. This is because my family lives 1,000 miles away. I wrote a long letter about how I knew at an early age. My coming out letter provided references. I gave them time to adjust to what they read before I asked how they felt. Direct face to face is ok. Test your environment so you know what the safest way may be to come out.

Check your method of coming out to ensure you feel it is right for you. Face to face may be the hardest because you will get their instant reactions. Most of the other ways allow your loved ones to understand their feelings. After some time has passed ask them if they have questions. Make sure you are ready for negative answers or challenging questions. If you prefer face to face, it might be best to dress androgynously. They will already have a lot to absorb.

Here are tips on coming out to parents:

· – Give yourself time to decide how to come and what you will say.
· – There are templates available for writing coming out letters. They may be helpful no matter how you come out.
· – Come out to the most supportive person in your life first.
· – Make sure you tell people this is who you are. You are not trying to hurt anyone or embarrass them.
· – Have reference material explaining what transgender is. Supply them a list of books, websites, etc. where they can find more information.
· – Allow them ample time to digest everything.
· – Do not assume a person's reaction. People may react differently to the way they live their lives or how they feel.

It is common during coming out to have negative feelings. We will go over some of these feelings.

Guilty - You may feel guilty coming out. Transitioning is personal. You may look selfish in other eyes. Your happiness counts. It is not selfish.

Scared - Feeling scared is natural. This time in your life may be exhilarating. You are entering an unknown area of people's feelings and reactions.

Uncertain - Uncertainty comes from not knowing what might happen. There is no way to know what will happen when you come out to friends, family, and other loved ones. The uncertainty can also cause confusion.

Unsafe - Stigmas may limit your ability to be out. Your living arrangements, location, and family acceptance may make it unsafe. You can prepare for this as much as you want but this goes back to the uncertainty. Have a backup plan.

Proud - Being proud of who you are becoming is a wonderful feeling. Be proud. Few people achieve this feeling.

Brave - People will say you have courage or bravery. I never felt that way. My relief after 55 years. It takes courage, but a lot of transgender people will tell you they never felt this.

Relief - As pointed out in brave, you will feel relief. Relief to have everything on the table.

The following is a sample coming out letter. (mine) Do not use this word for word. Personalize them for your life, feelings, and experiences. You only get this one chance to come out. Be sure you say everything you want to say. Try to keep it positive but explain why you need to do this.

If your family and friends saw no signs, explain why you found it hard to express yourself. Be honest about your feelings. Be honest about any depression or suicidal thoughts you may have. The depression and suicidal thoughts are why the transgender person is coming out and transitioning.

I do not know how to say this, so I will start with a little history. Ever since I was a kid, (about three or four) I have dressed up as a female from time to time. This carried on into adulthood. About seven years ago Sharon asked me about it and I dressed more. Throughout my life I have known I am a female. This is something I have needed to do since realizing how I was different. The time has come for me to share something with you that is personal. This is soon to become public. I share with a small percentage of people a clinical condition known as "Gender Dysphoria". I am transgender. This means that my inner gender identity as a female is inconsistent with my birth sex, as a male. Gender dysphoria is a clinical condition which has established and effective medical care. I never felt my existence as a male was right.

I have heard throughout my life about males at birth transitioning to females. I always knew this was possible to do. But I also knew the stereotypes I would walk into if I started my transition. Then I had time to meet two trans women who had started their transition. They were and still are happy. I spent from [month] to [month] trying to justify why I should not transition. All I came up with was that I should and could. I decided it was time for my happiness and feeling right.

On my birthday I took a testosterone blocker and female hormones. These are changing my body, and it will get to where I cannot hide it. I have been living as a woman almost 100 percent since January. I still have depression, and always will. The changes to my body so far have made me happier than I was. The changes are softening of the skin, redistribution of fat to make my butt bigger, and hips more defined. Also, the growth of breasts. I had my ears pierced in January and wear women's earrings all the time. This is something I have needed my whole life. I am glad I did this. When I present as a female I am at peace with the world. It feels so right. I am complete. I am not gay. My name is [name], and plans are to change my name soon.

This is not a passing thing or a fix for the depression. This is for me so I can be at peace with myself. If I don't do it, the thoughts of suicide may get worse again. I know this is a lot to take in, but I hope you still accept me.

Go to the following link for more information on being trans:
http://en.wikipedia.org/wiki/Gender_identity_disorder
Go to the following link for more information on hormones:
http://transhealthmodule.com/hormones.html

PART THREE

Transgender Children

CHAPTER ONE: IS MY CHILD TRANSGENDER?

"Rejecting your gay or transgender child won't make them straight. It will only mean you will lose them."
—Christina Engela, *Inanna Rising: Women Forged in Fire*

Being a kid and fitting in is hard enough. When they do not fit in, other kids harass and bully them. When a child comes out and starts their social transition, the harassment can distress them. They need all the help and support they can get from their loved ones. If your child is older, they have a better idea of what troubles may lie ahead with from being out. Transgender children may find going to school is the hardest thing they do. Bullying may drive them away from school, or worse. Parents should ensure the environment at school is right for them to thrive. If their bathroom policy is opposite what they need, the parents may want to find another school.

If your young child comes up to you and says "I know my gender. It is the same as my sex at birth," you do not question that statement. If your child comes up and says, "I know my gender and it differs from my sex at birth" your response may be "How do you know so young?" The answer is that your child will know their gender by age six at the latest. For many children, they know by three or four.

How can they know so young? How do I know for sure my child is transgender? What should I do if my child exhibits activities or wants to dress as the opposite gender? These are all great questions and this book will address these questions and more.

There are children coming out now as young as two or three years old. This may seem young for someone to know their gender. The reality is children notice at an early age they differ from other children.

How do children know so young they are not the correct gender? They know. But there is more to it. Many transgender individuals knew at an early age something was different. They may recognize this difference before others and recognize it right away. But this is not enough to say they are transgender. Watch for certain signs in a child. Even at this young age, it can influence their mental state.

Here are the signs:

•—**Persistent:** If a child is very persistent they are not their gender someone declared them at birth, they could be transgender. This persistence can come in many forms such as stating who they are, continuous statements like "Put me back in mommy's tummy so I can come back out right," or maybe praying to God to take them to heaven so they can come back right.
•—**Consistent:** If they are consistent in their message to the family in who they are, playing with the other gender's toys or the other gender.
•—**Insistent:** If they are very insistent in who they are and in the gender they are.

For many older transgender people, they may have known at an early. But their realization was at a time in history when being transgender or gay could mean you may lose your life. This still exists today but is not as bad as the 1960s and 1970s. In the last 10 years, the transgender community has made great strides. Some of our forward movement has slowed but children feel comfortable enough to come out.

This section goes over how you may know when your child is transgender. This subject may be the most important in this book.

We cover some of the problems you and your transgender child may confront at school. Speaking of school, we will discuss the problems with bullying and school.

It is also important for the child and their parents to seek support from like-minded people. When a parent talks to someone transgender or parents of a transgender child it can relieve their minds and anxiety. They may answer questions and help navigate the maze of being transgender.

If your child comes out before puberty, once puberty starts, they may want to start puberty blockers. This stops puberty to allow the child to mature enough to decide on taking hormones. Ensure they know when they start hormones many of the effects are not reversible.

Starting hormones without the change's puberty presents helps in becoming congruent. This makes their future easier. For an assigned male at birth, (AMAB) their voice will not drop. Trying to change your voice once it drops can be next to impossible for some. For an assigned female at birth, (AFAB) their breasts will not develop. Their voice will drop after they start hormone treatment and body and facial hair will grow.

By not allowing puberty blockers, it may cost them more for their transition and make it harder. Puberty blockers only delay puberty until they can decide and understand the effects of hormones. Give them the chance to be who they are. If they find they are not transgender they can stop the blockers and continue puberty.

What happens if I reject my child and kick them out of the house or they run away? This subject is important for the parents to know what can happen if the adolescent ends up on the street. These are facts, so you have a better understanding of what can happen.

Transgender children rejected by their parents are three times more likely to experience homelessness. They are 73 percent more likely to face incarceration. and 59 percent more likely to try suicide. The National Transgender Discrimination Survey found that transgender people are four times more likely to live in extreme poverty. Rejecting your child can affect their social-emotional health. It can also have lasting effects for the rest of their life. These are some of the statistics of what the transgender population faces daily. It is important to love and accept your child. <1>

They also need love and support because the few rights the transgender community had gained are eroding. This makes a life for your transgender child a lot harder. When they grow up and are on their own, their ability to survive gets even harder. If you do your best in supplying them with a safe place to be their self, it will help them later in life.

<1> https://www.vox.com/identities/2016/5/13/17938118/transgender-children-transitioning-parenting, Vox, @germanrlopez, german.lopez@vox.com, Updated Nov 14, 2018, 4:06pm EST

CHAPTER TWO: PARENTS SHOULD RESOLVE THEIR FEELINGS BEFORE RESPONDING

"What's more difficult? Accepting your child for who they are or having them die because you couldn't?"
—Anonymous

Try not to show your first emotions when your child comes out. Some family members reactions maybe negative. Your first response can have a lasting effect on your child and their future well-being.

Parents should educate themselves and resolve how they feel. Initial responses tend to not be a person's true feelings. This is important because being transgender is a challenging thing to endure. If you respond with an attitude your child may think they cannot be themselves, this can lead them to run away or take their life.

I know many religions are against transgender people. Parents need to resolve their religious beliefs. Children can feel trapped when they know who they are, but their parents are not responding. If their gender dysphoria is bad when they come out, they may be suicidal. That may be enough to push them over the edge.

Your response can also affect their ability to perform well at school and in life. If they have any depression at all, negativity may multiply those feelings.

Do not change your child. It is not possible to change who they are. Do not send your child to reparative therapy (aka conversion therapy or ex-gay therapy). I plead with you to reconsider. They tout reparative therapy changes a person from gay to straight, or transgender to cisgender. There are many ways they try to carry out this practice. This does not work and never has worked. Transgender and gay people are born this way, you cannot change them.

There are national organizations who stand by their statements that reparative therapy is ineffective and not ethical. It may even make current mental health problems your child has worse. They can even become psychotic.

I have Facebook friends who have gone through reparative therapy. Their mental state is worse. Reparative therapy facilities disqualify their identity and invalidate it.

If a child thinks their parents will not accept them, they may cross-dress to relieve some of the anxiety and depression. This may continue into their adult life.

Gay or lesbian people may hide their orientation. When a transgender person comes out their expression is visible. The parents may think they are losing their son, but they are gaining a daughter. (or losing a daughter but gaining a son) This is hard to accept for some, but it is better to have a live child than a dead one.

A child or adult will be happier when they can express their gender. They stay the same person on the inside. It is the outside of the transgender person who changes. Outside appearances do not make a person. People are who they feel they are in their heart. If they were caring and loving, they will still care and love. More so because they are happier.

Try to learn as much about being transgender as you can. This will make both you and your child's life easier. Learn the correct words to use and the steps for the transition. Also, learn about the oppression and how it affects the transgender community. This allows you to understand the difficulties your child is going through so you can be there to help them.

You can show your true acceptance of your child by becoming an advocate for the transgender community. By being an advocate, you are also helping your child to have a better and brighter future. It also will make you feel good on the inside.

CHAPTER THREE: RISKS YOUR TRANSGENDER CHILD MAY FACE

"Nothing prepares the parent of a transgender child, and nothing prepares that child. For me that's the good news: there's no rulebook."
—Nancy Moore

Even if you accept your transgender child and love them, there are still risks they take by being transgender. It is important to realize in our current society walking out the door transgender is a risk.

Transgender children take puberty blockers to pause puberty. This allows them time to mature before making any choice of taking hormones.

For transgender females, this can mean a difference between having a higher voice or a lower voice. This allows them to stop their beard from starting. The hormones stop it. The only ways to stop a beard after that is through laser hair removal or electrolysis.

When a transgender person assigned male at birth goes through puberty the only way to change any facial changes is with surgery. It is important to allow your child the freedom of expression and for them to delay their puberty.

Transgender females look like cisgender females. Transgender males look like cisgender males when they can use puberty blockers.

Transitioning while in school is hard as kids harass and bully more. Their life after school will be less stressful and more meaningful. School teachers and administrators may also harass your child. Many school districts do not allow a gender variant person to use the correct facilities.

The risks your child may take if you do not accept them are endless. Transgender youth may feel their true gender is essential to life and living. By withholding their ability to be themselves they may run away and live on the streets. They could also turn to drugs or alcohol to relieve the anxiety and stress they may feel. And their risk of suicide is higher.

Because of discrimination, transgender people find it harder to find a job. Dropping out of school can also affect their ability to find a job. Transgender females may find the sex industry is their only way to survive. There is a market for underage LGBTQ children. By working the sex industry, they may reason it is easier to start and move forward on their transition. Do not let your child become a statistic.

Working in the sex industry provides a higher risk of STD's. In the transgender female community, HIV is at epidemic levels. Your child becomes a higher risk of homicide on the streets.

If a transgender person cannot see a doctor, they may turn to the street or internet to get their hormones. This practice can be dangerous. Like illicit drugs, you never know what they may have cut with the hormones. Qualified health professionals are the only ones to administer hormones.

Transgender females may also turn to non-medical ways to get silicon injections to feminize their bodies. If they do not do this through qualified medical procedures, something could go wrong. Some silicon may be industrial grade. Industrial grade silicon is not acceptable for injecting in the human body.

CHAPTER FOUR: WHEN YOU REALIZE THEIR GENDER IDENTITY

"I'm the boy who has to tell his parents
he's not their little girl."
—Anonymous

Many people think children cannot know their gender until later in their childhood. They think their ability to realize their gender has not evolved enough. The fact is they only need to understand the difference between male and female. Some consider it to be child abuse allowing a child to express their correct gender. Some people are against children under 18 taking medications to stop puberty. They are also against taking hormones to start their medical transition. These interventions allow a child to be themselves and are not harmful.

You cannot change your child's gender identity. Whether by denial, punishment, ignoring, hoping it goes away, or reparative therapy it is not possible to change a person's gender. Your child will need your validation and support. Parents may want to have their child subjected to reparative therapy. Many organizations have proclaimed reparative therapy dangerous to the person subjected to it. It may have negative effects on their mental wellness. If you are thinking of using this therapy, please do not. Educate yourself on reparative therapy through proper websites. A section at the back supplies organizations that repudiate reparative therapy claims. This will give the parent a better idea of what it is and why it is dangerous.

So, how do they know so young? A child's surroundings, siblings, parents, and environment mold who they are at an early age. By two or three years old they can understand male or female among many other things.

If you are unsure whether your child is transgender, it is best to take them to a gender therapist. They have the knowledge to help the parents in understanding. They can also help the child understand their feelings.

The earlier a child expresses their in-congruency in their gender the better the chance they are transgender. They may express as their correct gender once they start puberty. There are children who will play with the other gender and the other gender's toys. This does not mean they are transgender. You should not restrict your child in their gender expression. Restricting them could have negative results such as self-hatred, depression and anxiety, and a sense of not belonging. <1>

How does a parent know it is not a phase? There is no way to tell. Most people have a sense of their gender between two and four years old. <1> This awareness stays stable over time, not wavering back and forth. Their identity becomes further refined at puberty onset and after puberty.

Current research does not show if a child who stops expressing as the opposite gender comes out transgender later in life. <1>

If they stay gender-expansive after about nine or ten years old (start of puberty) their identity may not change throughout their life.

For those parents who are not happy their child is transgender, they need to understand this is not reversible. You cannot "teach" the correct gender. Would you try to force a cisgender child to be transgender? By doing this it puts excessive pressure on the child to conform. This can cause them to have hatred towards their own body. This hatred often leads to eating disorders, self-mutilation, and suicide.

In the words of Harvey Milk, "All young people, regardless of sexual orientation or identity, deserve a safe and supportive environment in which to achieve their full potential." Harvey Milk was born in New York. He moved to San Francisco in 1972. Harvey had three unsuccessful attempts for a political seat. In 1977 he ran for and won city supervisor. Milk, along with the other supervisors passed a non-discrimination bill in San Francisco. Milk spent 11 months in office when on November 27, 1978, Dan White assassinated Milk and Mayor Moscone. Dan White was another city supervisor who had resigned. He tried to get his seat back.

<1> - Trans-Parenting FAQ. (n.d.). Retrieved from Trans-Parenting: http://www.trans-parenting.com/understanding-gender/faq/

CHAPTER FIVE: ALLOW YOUR CHILD THE FREEDOM TO EXPRESS THEIR GENDER

"I stand for freedom of expression, doing what you
believe in and going after your dreams."
—Madonna Ciccone

This is not about you and any embarrassment you may perceive. This is about a scared child hoping you will continue to understand, love, and care for them. Remember this. Any attempt to resist who they may be can have catastrophic circumstances.

Whether your child is three years old or in their teens it is important to allow them the freedom to be themselves. No matter what they may express as when you repress what they feel you may risk their mental health. If they succeed in suicide this would devastate most parents.

Their depression and anxiety may limit their ability to live a happier life. Do not force them to repress their feelings, their gender dysphoria may get worse. Some assigned male at birth people has had gender dysphoria bad enough they try to remove their penis.

As a transgender person myself I know a parent can feel devastated by their child coming out as transgender. Many transgender people feel better and happier when they can express their known gender. They are less likely to have bad mental health problems when loved and accepted at home and in school. This is important to their existence. Children who can express their gender in school well and have a higher rate of graduating.

Older children may run away from home to express themselves. Forty percent of all runaways on the street are LGBTQ, and many of those end up in the sex industry. It forces them into the sex industry, or it may be the only way for them to survive.

I hope most parents would want a live female child instead of a dead male child, or vice-versa. This is a reality for many LGBTQ children because they cannot be themselves. Think before you act. It may save your child from a rough and scary life or in the worst case, death.

One thing a parent should never do is to insist on their child transition. This is their decision and they will let you know when they feel comfortable enough. Their mental health and happiness are of utmost importance during this time. Some may start their social transition at once. Others may stall to ensure safety for them. Remember, this is your child. They are not doing this to embarrass or hurt you. This is a scary time for them, and they need all the help you can give.

CHAPTER SIX: TRANSGENDER CHILDREN AND SCHOOL

"I wouldn't change myself at all. Being transgender is who I am: a strong person, a confident person. Being transgender gives me my personality."
—Jazz Jennings

Some schools are better than others, but some remain non-accepting. This may not be true for your child's school. Bullying, bigotry, and discrimination may still exist. There are schools teaching diversity to both the faculty and the students. By educating people it becomes clearer to them what being transgender is.

There will always be bullies no matter how much education they get. Through education, more people are understanding. This helps when a transgender child needs help stopping a bully.

If your child is getting bullied, alert the school's supervision. This may stop further bullying. When you confront a bully, they stop bullying.

Bathroom bills. Bathroom bills are legislation our governments have been trying to pass to restrict transgender people's use of bathrooms to our sex assigned at birth. I talk more on this subject later in the book, but I want to discuss a little here why they are harmful. There is a suicide hotline for transgender people. Transgender people run the hotline. They have a better idea of what transgender people go through. If a legislative session enters a bathroom bill or made a law, the calls to the Trans Lifeline double. [1]

After reports of a Trump memo saying they would redefine gender the calls to the Trans Lifeline quadrupled. Ensure you know what negativity is going on against the transgender community. It may influence your child's well-being. [2]

When not allowed to use the correct bathroom, a transgender child's gender dysphoria may rise. It can cause other physical problems. I will go into more in the section on bathroom bills.

The U.S. Government does not have a law for anti-bullying. They might cover bullying under other federal laws depending on the protected class status of the person being bullied.

All 50 states have anti-bullying laws. Some states also have anti-cyberbullying laws in place. Some states may need each school district to adopt their own anti-bullying plan. If your child faces bullying by school-mates at school or not, report it to the school's administration. Children take their lives every day because of bullying. Bullying can be worse for a transgender child. Protect them. They have only one life.

If a person states they are transgender, believe them. Being transgender is not the current fad or style. There are people who hate transgender people without even knowing one. It is hard enough for a transgender person to come out. Most children and youth do not want other students to see their genitalia. Transgender people go to great lengths to ensure others see nothing they should not. Transgender people use the restroom for the same thing's others do; the toilet, freshening up, applying makeup and other things. They are not in there to cause a problem.

Schools which have no transgender students should still ensure they have procedures in place. This makes it easier when they get their first transgender child. This helps parents know they are an accepting school delivering a safe place for transgender students. There is also the case of correct pronouns and names. Make sure the administration and staff know and use correct names and pronouns. It is imperative a child can walk into a school and learn with as little stress and harassment as possible.

<1> https://www.thedailybeast.com/after-north-carolinas-law-trans-suicide-hotline-calls-double, The Daily Beast, Samantha Allen, 04.20.16 1:00 AM ET
<2> https://www.newsweek.com/after-trump-admin-memo-moves-define-gender-trans-lifeline-receives-4x-amount-1195253, Newsweek, Jenni Fink, 10/31/18 AT 11:09 AM

CHAPTER SEVEN: SEEK LIKE-MINDED SUPPORT. HERE'S WHY

"It matters not what someone is born,
but what they grow to be."
—Albus Dumbledore

One of the most helpful things parents can do for their child is to seek support. It is not a bad idea for the parents to find support themselves. This allows everyone to talk to people who are going through the same trials and tribulations. There are local support groups for transgender people. They may only be for those over 18. Facebook groups have like-minded individuals going through the same thing. This may also be a way to meet up with other families and allow your child to meet other transgender children.

This support can be vital when everything may seem to fall apart. Having a friend who understands what you are going through can be exhilarating. There are many other transgender and non-binary groups on Facebook. One group for parents is Serendipity-Do-Dah (Mama Bears). This group is private, and you must know someone to become a part of the group.

There are other resources to help your transgender child in their journey. These resources may answer the questions the parents have.

There is an organization called Parents, Families, and Friends of Lesbians and Gays (PFLAG) which has over 400 local chapters. They have meetings once a month. In larger urban areas they may have a weekly meeting.

There is an app available called Meetup. It is a service supplying a principal place to list local meetups of all kinds. They have local meetings for LGBTQ people depending on the size of the area you live in. It may be a handy app to have on your phone. You can select specific subjects of interest including LGBTQ meetings. Find transgender-specific groups to get the perspective you need at a time you need it most.

At the back of this book are references. Included are organizations who supply support. There are advocacy organizations, also. Please use it if you feel stuck and do not know where to turn.

CHAPTER EIGHT: I AM ON THE STREET! WHAT CAN HAPPEN?

"I was human. I am human now. Being transgender
doesn't make me any less human."
—Anonymous

The transgender community has the highest rate of suicide attempts at 41 percent. That is 10 times higher than the attempts by the total population. <1> This statistic is not for adolescents. It stands for adult attempts during their life. Thus, it is imperative to love, support, and accept your transgender child. This would mean 574,000 transgender people in their life have at least once tried suicide. They base this on 0.6 percent of the United States population or 1.4 million transgender people.

For many adolescents on their own on the streets, they may find it hard to survive. They may find the sex trade the easiest way to survive. The only problem with this is they may find themselves stuck in the sex trafficking industry.

Once they end up in the sex trafficking business, they may find it hard to escape. Many who run these rings rule by controlling people and using their manipulating tricks to instill fear.

Forty-six percent of homeless LGBTQ youth ran away from home because of family rejection. Seventeen percent ended up on the streets when they aged out of the foster care system. Within 48 hours of running away, one in three kids will end up recruited into commercial sexual exploitation. This includes streetwalking and online sex trades. <2>

It is not child abuse to allow them to start puberty blockers upon puberty and to start hormones when they feel ready. It is child abuse to throw your child on the streets and have them go through the hell they face out there.

Note: They use Puberty blockers for children who start their puberty to early. In recent times doctors have been using them as an off-product medication to block puberty in transgender children. This allows the child to mature and give them the ability to make a more informed decision to start hormones. By blocking puberty, the child can go through the correct puberty matching their gender identity.

<1> https://www.usatoday.com/story/news/nation/2015/08/16/transgender-individuals-face-high-rates--suicide-attempts/31626633/, USA Today, Laura Ungar, Aug. 16, 2015

<2> https://www.washingtonpost.com/news/parenting/wp/2017/03/29/homeless-rates-for-lgbt-teens-are-alarming-heres-how-parents-can-change-that/?noredirect=on&utm_term=.b9de6879ea2b, The Washington Post, By Jaimie Seaton, March 29, 2017

CHAPTER NINE: SEX TRAFFICKING OF TRANSGENDER CHILDREN

"Of the 1,345 documented incidences of human trafficking in the U.S. last year, 973 of them were related to sex trafficking."
—Polaris Project

There are parents who ask their transgender children to leave home. The reasons vary. For some of these children, to survive, many turn to the sex trade. Some join while others are forced to work in the sex trade. They under report sex trafficking of transgender, like many other things. By one account, 40 percent of all kids on the street are LGBTQ. <1> This is very disproportionate because less than five percent of the population is LGBTQ. <2>

Transgender friends or family may victimize children. This leaves them vulnerable to sex traffickers. Children who run away from abusive homes may find the streets to be worse.

LGBTQ youth victimized sexually is 58.7 percent vs. 33.4 percent of heterosexual and cisgender homeless youth. A stunning 67 percent of transgender youth have engaged in sex work. Even if they volunteer to go into sex work, they may end up at sex traffickers mercy. <3>

If you think a child may be in the sex trade and/or manipulated by sex traffickers, ensure you contact the proper authorities. Listed below is the hotline to for those wanting to get out of human trafficking and to report human trafficking.

National Human Trafficking Hotline
Call: 1-888-373-7888 help@humantraffickinghotline.org

Polaris Project is a wonderful source of sex trafficking. They supply insight, resources, and help for those who looking for someone or someone looking to get out. https://polarisproject.org

<1> – https://www.washingtonpost.com/news/parenting/wp/2017/03/29/homeless-rates-for-lgbt-teens-are-alarming-heres-how-parents-can-change-that/?utm_term=.83fa4c936975, The Washington Post, Jaimie Seaton, March 29, 2017

<2> – https://en.wikipedia.org/wiki/LGBT_demographics_of_the_United_States, Wikipedia
<3> – https://polarisproject.org/resources/sex-trafficking-and-lgbtq-youth, Polaris Project, Valerie Schmitt, May 2016

PART FOUR

Transitioning

THE FACTS
(about transgender kids)

CHAPTER ONE: SHOULD I TRANSITION?

"Be who you want to be, not what
others want to see."
—G. AVETIS

No one can answer the above question except you. This question is personal and only you can answer it. People may help in your journey ensuring your safety and have the resources to transition. I will offer you the tools to help find your answer. If you transition remember this discovery is yours. If you find you are transgender, transitioning is not a must. Everyone's transition looks different. If you do not suffer from gender dysphoria or it does not affect your mental health, you may not need to transition.

I am transgender and I would never wish for someone to be transgender. It can make for a tough life. it has been well worth it. If you do not want people to stare, laugh, or bully you, do not transition. I do not want to scare you into not transitioning. I want you to get as much knowledge as possible.

Even if they had a blue pill to turn a person male or a pink pill to turn them female, my choice is always the pink pill. This is because I am a female. If your decision to transition is yes, you may find you feel regret from time to time. It will get to where those thoughts will not even come. Those thoughts do not last long, and they subside the longer you are out. If you transition, do not let these thoughts stop you. Everyone gets them. They happen when things get tough.

Make sure you take a few things into consideration. If you live in a rural region, people may accept you less. Some rural areas are worse than others. Urban areas will have more accepting and understanding people.

If you believe your parents will not accept you being transgender, it may be best to wait. If you are unsure, test the waters. Tell them a story of a fictitious transgender friend. Grasp how they respond. By doing this you get an idea for their mindset on transgender people. Though you can be yourself on the streets, the street is a dangerous place for a transgender person.

For a variety of transgender people, the decision to transition may be live or die. If you are contemplating suicide because of your gender dysphoria it may be best to tell your parents you are transgender and tell them your feelings. Remember someone somewhere will supply help or support. Reach out and do not take your life.

This may appear to be the worst thing to happen, and it may be, but things will get better. Just give it time.

There may be reasons social transition is your limit. Physical health may restrict your ability to take medications or have surgeries. The social transition can be a lifesaver. Remember, your choices are greater than what you think. Consider all offerings.

To be yourself can lift your spirits. If you face roadblocks and you are not sure where to turn, try to find help. There may be an easier answer than you think.

I am transgender with severe MDD. (major depressive disorder) Life gets better. My gender dysphoria made my depression much worse. My decision was no decision. I wanted to live. I love you, and so do many others. Do not let depression get the best of you.

As a transgender person if you suffer from gender dysphoria and depression, write your triggers on paper. By realizing your triggers, it will be easier to avoid them If you transition. Come back to your list from time to time. You may find your list helpful. It might give you the knowledge of what you need to concentrate on.

Trans Lifeline: US: 877-565-8860 Canada: 877-330-6366

CHAPTER TWO: WHEN THE DECISION TO TRANSITION IS NO LONGER A DECISION

"My transition has felt like burning every bridge I have ever known and swimming across the river alone."
—Anonymous

Being transgender is not a decision. We are born this way, so the decision is to transition to our internal felt gender. Whew, cleared that up. Who wants to face bullying, being discriminated against, marginalized, and oppressed? You are a wonderful person with a special gift which few people receive. You will be your authentic self. Take it and run with it. You will not regret it.

If gender dysphoria and depression is bad, transition may be your only choice. Restricting your ability to transition can trigger suicidal thoughts. The inability to be yourself may be the trigger.

You will hear me repeat this throughout this book because I lived it. Do not let your gender dysphoria take your life. Be who you recognize you are. Walk out the door with your head high and be proud. We love you and we want the best for you. Please, call someone to get help or to talk if you are beyond planning your suicide and are preparing.

If you are under 18, this can be hard to continue going through. As an adult you can become who you are, circumstances allowing. Older transgender people go through most of their lives before they got to be themselves.

If you realize you are transgender, this decision is only to transition. If you realize you are transgender, you have always been transgender.

CHAPTER THREE: TRANSGENDER PEOPLE FIND DISCOMFORT WITH THEIR BODIES

"Celebrate the idea that you don't fit in.
Find your own fit. Stay unique."
—Betsey Johnson

Cisgender people see the correct person in the mirror. Transgender individuals see someone foreign to what their mind informs them. Many transgender people dislike mirrors because they lie to us.

Once you have started hormone replacement therapy (HRT) you will see the positive changes to your body. These may be facial hair and a deeper voice for transgender males. For transgender females, it may be breast development and the reduction in body hair.

Hormones can change emotions and well-being for transgender people. It may be what your body needs. This can be an exhilarating time for the transgender individual.

Even though you may achieve congruency, the gender dysphoria may stay. For a transgender female, facial air may trigger gender dysphoria. It may happen when looking in the mirror and still seeing the other genders body parts remaining. For a transgender male, the sight of their breasts can be a source for gender dysphoria.

Once on hormones, most transgender people find their gender dysphoria subsides. Remember, you are on a journey and only you who can call it complete. Everyone's life is a constant transition. Transgender people are doing more transitioning in a shorter time.

When a person's body is not congruent with what their brain says, it may be at a point of triggering suicide attempts. By achieving congruence, you may find extreme relief in the darkness you may have lived in for years.

CHAPTER FOUR: THE REALITY OF ACHIEVING YOUR TRUE GENDER IDENTITY

"It's easy to fictionalize an issue when you're not aware of the many ways in which you are privileged by it."
—Kate Bornstein, Gender Outlaws: The Next Generation

One thing to keep in mind, you are you and no one can tell you otherwise. During your journey, you will encounter bumps in the road. You may encounter negative reactions along the way. If you love yourself, your journey will have a positive impact on your life.

When you love yourself, you will realize the love you may have for humanity. Allow no one to spoil these wondrous feelings. If people cannot accept you as you are, and they say toxic words to you, cut them from your life. This may be harder if you live at home. To live your life with happiness, you may have people you may need to remove from your life. This may appear harsh, but to survive, sometimes you need to get rid of those who you thought loved you, and who you loved. Love does not mean acceptance.

Your happiness is most important. For many transgender people, toxic people can affect any depression they have. Anyone who has had depression can tell you this. It is frustrating and tiring being attacked. If they love you, they might realize what they are doing to you and become more accepting and loving of you.

When you can look in the mirror and the correct reflection is there, you will know your journey is well worth it. You may find this overwhelming. Cry! I did. The family does not have to be blood. People who love you for you will find you and appreciate your wonderful qualities. Stick in there and walk tall. You should be proud of who you are becoming.

PART FIVE

Religion

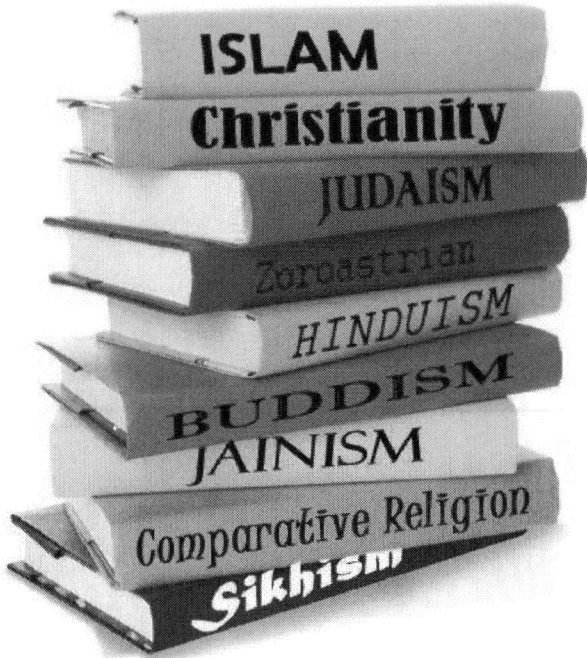

CHAPTER ONE: RELIGION

Nature chooses who will be transgender,
individuals don't choose this.
—MERCEDES RUEHL

I included religion because religious values are a part of many transgender individuals lives. When I was 17 I stopped going to church due to problems endured because of religion. I found my way back to church after I came out as a transgender woman. It had been 40 years between stopping religion and starting again.

Because you are transgender or LGBQ, does not mean you need to stop attending church. It may mean to continue going to church you will need to find a new church. Many religions will allow you into their church as a visitor but may not allow you to become a member. If this is how they treat you, they may also preach on how you are committing a sin being transgender. I will not give my opinion. My belief is everyone should have their own religious beliefs and values.

If you need to change churches or find a new one there are ways to find one without attending.

1. – Search on Wikipedia for affirming religions. If you know which religions may affirm, it may make your next part easier.

a. – Once you find an affirming religion on Wikipedia, try to find a local church of that religion. Email the minister to confirm the church is affirming. If they are, ask if you can talk to the minister about their beliefs of gender identity and being transgender. If you can stop the unpleasantries, it may save anxiety.

2. – A website called http://www.churchclarity.com has a database of churches. They rate them by inclusiveness. If you find an affirming church not yet listed, you can enter information and they will assess that information. You can also search by your area to find a local affirming church. Church Clarity's database is far from complete. Do not feel frustrated if they have no churches in your area.

CHAPTER TWO: WORLD RELIGIONS AND THEIR INCLUSIVENESS

"We are trying to construct a more inclusive society. We are going to make a society in which no one is left out."
—Franklin D. Roosevelt

I wanted to provide this chapter for reference to some of the world's more well-known religions. The information below is current as of this writing. If a religion is not inclusive, it does not mean a local church of that religion is not inclusive. Always check with local churches for your personal religion.

For many religions on this list, it may be a church by church or diocese by diocese decision.

1.—Christian Church (Disciples of Christ)—In 2013 the General Assembly voted to affirm and welcome LGBTQ people. This included taking part in all areas of church life, including leadership. This does not dictate policy for all congregations. They encourage individual congregations to become more inclusive.

2.—Conservative Judaism—They have taken a firm stance on a total inclusion. They extended their previous in 2011 for a total inclusion to include the transgender community.

a.—In 2016, the Rabbinical Assembly passed a historic resolution on affirming the rights of transgender and non-conforming people. This affirmed its commitment to the full welcome, acceptance, and inclusion of all people. of all gender identities in Jewish life and general society. Your experience may vary from one synagogue to another.

3.—Islam—Sunni and Shi'a, Transgender people they may find it is rare within a mainstream mosque to feel comfortable.

a.—They recognize transgender men and women with many Islamic cultures around the world. As early as 1988, gender confirmation surgery is acceptable under Islamic law. After having the surgery, they may find that acceptance dwindle a little.

4.—Oriental Orthodox Church—Different churches within the Oriental Orthodoxy function as separate entities. They appear to come to a consensus on LGBTQ issues though.

a.—With transgender people, the church tends more towards the belief being transgender is biological.

5.—**Pentecostals**—They run to the conservative side believing being gay or transgender is a sin. There is a faction of the church called Reconciling Pentecostals International. They supply an affirming atmosphere within their congregations.

6.—**Episcopal Church**—In 1976 the Episcopal denomination, in both the House of Deputies and House of Bishops voted for an inclusive Episcopal Church. This included gender identity or expression. This law includes a reference to using the preferred name and pronouns.

7.—**Presbyterian Church (USA)**—The 223rd General Assembly of the Presbyterian Church (USA) voted in 2018 to affirm its commitment to the full welcome, acceptance, and inclusion of transgender people, people who identify as gender non-binary (gender non-conforming), and people of all gender identities within the full life of the church and the world.

a.—Your experience may differ between different congregations, but many congregations welcome and include you in their congregation.

8.—**Roman Catholic Church**—They have no specific policy for transgender congregates in the Roman Catholic Church. Know of their policy of acceptance of transgender people may vary from congregation to congregation. It may also vary between conservative and progressive areas.

9.—**Religious Society of Friends (Quakers)**—Many Quaker communities are open and welcoming to LGBTQ people. The Religious Society of Friends also supplies advocacy work for the LGBTQ community.

10.—**United Methodist Church**—The United Methodist Church splits on their views of transgender people. This split is 50/50. The religious laws of the United Methodist Church do not allow for an exclusive and affirming congregate. The UMC met in February 2019. They voted to continue not being affirming. It is hard to say what may happen to the UMC. If you are a part of the United Methodist Church and your congregation is not inclusive, look for another in your area which is inclusive.

11.—**Humanists**—The Humanist Church are committed activists for the LGBTQ community. The Humanist religion strives for fair treatment of the transgender community.

12.—**Unity**—Unity teaches people are created with sacred worth and no one exists outside the heart of God. Its basic principles state God is good, and because all people exist within God, they are good.

13.—**Reconstructionist Judaism**—Of the four leading Jewish denominations, the Reconstructionist Movement is the most welcoming and affirming. They welcome transgender individuals, accept transgender students to the Reconstructionist Rabbinical College and ordains transgender rabbis.

14.—**Orthodox Judaism**—This religion adheres to religious law. Some congregations believe being transgender is not a choice and provide acceptance and affirmation.

Like much other religion's beliefs on the LGBTQ community, Orthodox Judaism moves toward a progressive belief.

15.—**Hinduism**—The Hindu religion has no central authority, so attitudes between temples may vary.

16.—**Reform Judaism**—Reform Judaism welcomes transgender people. They allow for the ordination of transgender rabbis. They also encourage its communities to become inclusive of transgender individuals.

17.—**Alliance of Baptists**—Alliance of Baptists lists gender identities in its celebration of inclusivity. They are an affirming religion.

18.—**Presbyterian Church in America**—The Presbyterian Church in America has no official stance on being transgender. They include gender distortions on its list of sins.

19.—**Buddhism**—Within the teachings of Buddhism there is no mention of transgender people. This may be another religion which may differ from one temple to another.

20.—**Eastern Orthodox Church**—There is no formal treatment by a Council of Bishops on being transgender. They condemn gender confirmation surgery because of God's design for everyone.

21.—**Church of the Nazarene**—There is no stated policy on transgender inclusion.

22.—**Southern Baptist Convention**—In 2012 at the SBC's Annual Meeting, the SBC passed a resolution. They wrote gender identity as being determined by the sex assigned at birth (SAAB).

23.—**United Church of Christ**—The UCC welcoming and affirming of transgender people. Resolutions of the General Synod passed in 2003 invites all members to, "learn about the realities of transgender experience and expression, including the gifts and callings and needs of transgender people". Transgender and intersexual people are welcome as clergy and in lay leadership roles.

24.—**American Baptist Churches USA**—ABCUSA does not appear to address transgender issues.

25.—**Seventh-day Adventist Church**—The Seventh-day Adventist allow transgender people as members. They do not believe in gender confirmation surgery for those whose genitalia are male or female. For those who do not proceed with GCS, they allow them as members if they follow the church's beliefs on marriage and sexuality.

26.—**Evangelical Lutheran Church in America**—Gender Identity is included in the Evangelical Lutheran Churches "Human Sexuality: Gift and Trust" Social Statement. Social Statements set policy for the ELCA and guide its advocacy and works as an engaged church.

27.—**Unitarian Universalist Association**—The Unitarian Universalist Association (UUA) website, "We not only open our doors to people of all sexual orientations and gender identities, but we also value the diversity of sexuality and gender and see it as a spiritual gift. We create inclusive religious communities and work for LGBTQ justice and equity as a core part of who we are."

28.—Metropolitan Community Churches—MCC established its Transgender Ministries program to support church communities as they become more welcoming and affirming of transgender and gender non-conforming individuals.

29.—African Methodist Episcopal Church—The AME Church does not appear to address transgender issues but follows scriptural teachings about God's creation that gender identity is biological.

30.—National Baptist Convention USA Inc.—The National Baptist Convention has not released a formal statement on transgender members or their ordination.

There are more religions, but the list is too great to provide in this book. Remember, to feel comfortable, it may be best to find an affirming church.

There is also a group on Facebook which calls itself a transgender church. A transgender woman who lost her church because of her identity formed the group. It is possible to find a church right for you. If you find it causes anxiety you can always form spiritual practices on your own.

Note: Ordination is ordaining or conferring holy orders on someone.

PART SIX

Transitioning

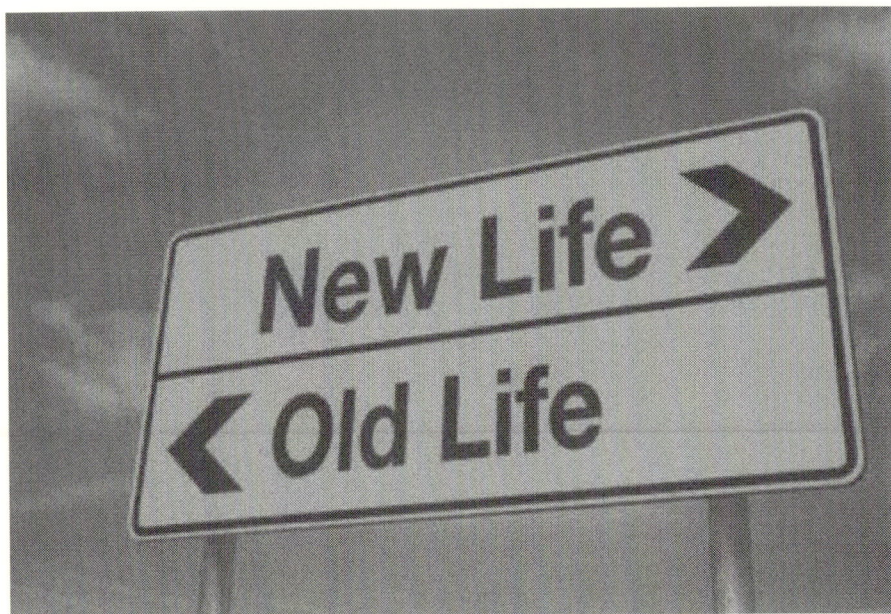

CHAPTER ONE: THE ROAD TO TRANSITION

I may have a beard, and manly limbs and body, yet
confined by these, I am and remain a woman.
—Karl Heinrich Ulrichs

There is an unlimited number of ways to transition including not transitioning. Just be you. Find comfort with your new self. Do steps before coming out. There is nothing wrong with that. This allows you to achieve come closer to congruence. Whether you do all steps and transition, this makes you no less transgender. Allow no one to tell you otherwise.

There are four main steps which make up most of a person's transition. These four steps impact the largest changes to your body to become your new self. Note there are 5 steps, but the two medical steps are one. This is because one step is transgender females and the other step is transgender males.

The following is a list of the four steps and the processes they entail:

•—**Social transition**—You can start this step before coming out. You need not to be 24/7/365 when first starting transition. If you change your look at a slower pace it can keep from surprising people.

Transgender males may want to wear a binder and dress in males' clothes or the style they enjoy. Transgender females may want to buy breast forms (and a bra for them) if they will dress as a female. As with transgender males, the transgender female may want to find their style during this time.

Transgender females may want to grow their hair. Transgender females may want to practice at changing their voice. This is not an easy task. My voice remains male after five years. Laser hair removal and/or electrolysis for transgender females to remove any beard. There are many things the transgender individual can do during their social transition. There are too many to list here.

•—**Medical—Hormones,** You can start this step before coming out to loved ones. There is limited time before the effects of the hormones show. Therapists and endocrinologists following (WPATH) Standards of Care require a one-year real-life experience. This can restrict your ability to start hormones before coming out. It might be in your best interest to find a local clinic or Planned Parenthood. There are places which will provide hormones with informed consent. Appointments with them may take as long or longer than the one year wait.

•—**Medical—Top surgery (transgender males)**, The removal of transgender males' breast and reconstructing the nipple to make the torso more congruent. Even the 6,000 to 7,000-dollar cost for this surgery may be beyond certain budgets. Those able to afford this surgery find it relieves their gender dysphoria a little.

•—**Medical—Gender confirmation surgery (GCS)**, This surgery may be the most affirming for the transgender person. Also called bottom surgery. This surgery brings their primary sex characteristics in line with their gender. GCS is beyond most transgender people's budgets. Certain health insurance companies cover the surgery. GCS can be a life-saving and life-affirming intervention. Many cannot afford the co-pay. The average cost for a transgender female's GCS is $22,000. The average cost for a transgender male's surgery can run up to $100,000. Larger insurance companies carry policies which cover these surgeries. Make sure you know your co-pay ahead of time. There may be requirements to stay at a local hotel for up to a week to make sure no problems occur. Transgender females may get their breast enhancement done at the same time they do their GCS.

•—**Medical—Feminine facial surgery (FFS) (transgender females)**, This is plastic surgery to bring a transgender female's face into congruence. Few elect to get FFS due to costs and risks. For various transgender females, the changes to their face from the estrogen may be enough.

Understand that all surgeries come with a risk. I have heard stories of problems faced after surgery. Make sure you check the surgeon you select for successful surgeries. This step may save you pain on the back side. Even if your surgeon has a wonderful track record, problems may still occur.

CHAPTER TWO: HORMONE EFFECTS ON THE TRANSGENDER PERSON'S BODY

"It's not about being a new person but becoming the person you were already meant to be."
—Anonymous

Hormones are a wonderful thing. Many transgender people only do a social and hormone transition. At the back of the book in the reference section is a chart showing the main hormones taken by both transgender women and men. It shows the effects the hormones produce on the body. It is best to know before starting hormones. Particular effects may be undesirable for you.

For most, they find the effects the hormones bring them congruence to resolve some of the gender dysphoria. Know the effects before starting hormones. There are effects by the hormones you may not want. Below are the medications and how they affect the body.

Hormone replacement therapy (HRT) brings changes for congruence for the transgender person. Hormones deliver physical and emotional changes. All humans have testosterone, the masculinizing hormone, and estrogen, the feminizing hormone. Their primary sex characteristic determines which hormone is prominent for the person. Age, physical health, puberty, and a variety of other variables can change the number of hormones produced. Transgender women who have not had GCS or an orchiectomy use an anti-androgen. Anti-androgens block testosterone. To raise their estrogen level, they take estrogen. Progesterone is a choice for a few transgender women. Progesterone supplies feminizing effects.

Note: Orchiectomy is a surgical procedure to remove the testes. Transgender females get this to stop producing testosterone. If they are not getting GCS, they may do this. They perform it if the transgender female's GCS is a few years off and they want to stop the testosterone production.

Transgender men need only testosterone. Testosterone is strong and will lower the transgender male's estrogen to acceptable levels. <1>

We will first cover the hormones transgender women use for the feminization of their face and bodies.

•—**Anti-androgens** They make anti-androgens for various other medical conditions, including:

    †—**Spironolactone**—Spironolactone is the main anti-androgen used by transgender women. They make spironolactone for use as a diuretic. It reduces water in the body for those with high blood pressure or heart failure. They use spironolactone to treat swelling (edema) caused by a variety of conditions. (heart failure and liver disease) It removes excess fluid and improves symptoms.

    They use spironolactone to treat low potassium levels, and for conditions in which the body is making too much of a natural chemical (aldosterone).

    †—**Flutamide**—They use this with other medications to treat particular prostate cancers. They may select Flutamide if side effects of the other anti-androgens are bothersome.

    †—**Finasteride**—This anti-androgen blocks producing testosterone. It may reduce male pattern baldness. They market Finasteride as an anti-balding medication. Transgender women take Finasteride when side effects of spironolactone are bothersome.

Anti-androgens may cause gynecomastia; growth of a male's breast tissue. The reduction in testosterone causes this. The doctor will prescribe them to lower testosterone. This allows lower levels of estrogen usage. Estrogen in higher doses may cause heart attacks or strokes.

•—One to three months after starting an anti-androgen alone

    †—Decrease in sex drive.
    †—Fewer occurrences of waking up with an erection or having spontaneous erections.
    †—A few will find it difficult to achieve an erection even when aroused.
    †—Decreased ability to make sperm and ejaculatory fluid.
    †—Gradual changes and slower growth of facial and body hair, and slowing of male pattern baldness.

•—2 years after starting anti-androgens

    †—Slight breast growth (reversible sometimes).

Estrogen is the heart of medical transition for the transgender women. Because estragon changes many features of the transgender women's body. It is hard to select what affects you may want.

Estrogens feminizing effects are much stronger than anti-androgens on cells with estrogen receptors. It offers an indirect suppression of testosterone in the body.

This is a timeline and how estrogen affects the body:

•—One to three months after starting estrogen.

  †—Softening of skin.
  †—Decrease in muscle mass and an increase in body fat. Body fat produces a more feminine pattern (hips, butt, breast).
  †—Decrease in sex drive.
  †—Fewer occurrences of waking up with an erection or having spontaneous erections. Various transgender individuals may find their erections are less firm during sex or not erect.
  †—Decreased ability to make sperm and ejaculatory fluid.
  †—Gradual changes in nipple and breast growth.
  †—Slower growth of facial and body hair. It may also eradicate body hair.

•—One to two years after starting estrogen.

  †—Slowed or stopped male pattern balding.
  †—Decrease in testicular size.

The advantages of estrogen are:

•—Breast and nipple growth starts early. (within the first few months) Full grown can take two or more years to reach their full size. The time and size are unpredictable. Transgender women will suffer pain with their nipples and breast tissue. This shows the hormones are working. You find out how much you bump into your chest. Many transgender women achieve breasts one cup size smaller than their mom's or sisters. Surgeons may ask you to wait for breast enhancement until your breasts slow or stop growing. Tissue can lift between the breasts.

•—Transgender women's emotions are the first most notice. These emotions change quick and before six months. These emotions may take time to start. <1>

Transgender males take testosterone. Estrogen blockers are available. Most transgender males do not need estrogen blockers. Testosterone is strong enough to overcome a little of the estrogen.

Advantages of testosterone:

•—**Testosterone**—Testosterone comes in many forms. The most effective is shots and pellets (under the skin). They produce testosterone for use by cisgender men and women for varying conditions.

The physical changes to a transgender males' body from testosterone can be sexual and physical. How you administer testosterone can affect how fast the masculinization happens. It can affect emotional and physical health effects.

Transdermal patches take the longest for masculinization to occur. A transgender males' period will stop unless administering Andriol. Andriol does not have the same effects as testosterone, so most transgender males do not use it. Testosterone, when administered to transgender males, will stop their period for most. It is important to bank eggs if you plan to have children

Testosterone shots can influence their emotions. The cause is the excess of testosterone after the shot. Not having enough testosterone right before the next shot can change emotions. Other forms of testosterone affect their emotions less.

Changes when taking masculinizing hormones for transgender males:

•—One to three months after starting testosterone.

†—Increased sex drive.
†—Vaginal dryness.
†—Growth of the clitoris (around 1–3 cm).
†—Increased growth, coarseness, and thickness of hair on arms, legs, chest, back, and abdomen.
†—Oilier skin and increased acne.
†—Increased muscle mass and upper body strength.
†—Redistribution of body fat to a more "masculine" pattern (more fat around the waist, less around the hips).

•—Three to six months after starting testosterone.

†—Menstrual cycles stop.
†—Voice cracks and drops but can take a year to finish changing.

•—One or more years after starting testosterone.

†—Gradual growth of facial hair (one to four years from starting testosterone to reach full growth).

Doing surgery may be one of the last things the transgender individual will do. Surgeries are unobtainable for many transgender people. Insurance companies may cover affirming surgery. Their copays and other costs may make it too expensive, even with insurance.

<1>—https://apps.carleton.edu/campus/gsc/assets/hormones_MTF.pdf,   Carleton Education, February 2006 Vancouver Coastal Health, Transcend Transgender Support & Education

CHAPTER THREE: SURGERIES AND THE STEPS TO CONGRUENCE

"It's not about surgeries. It's the feeling we are complete."
—Stephania Kanitsch

You need not complete your transition. Only you know when you are complete. Surgeries are unobtainable for many. Insurance companies may cover affirming surgery. Their copays and other costs may make it too expensive, even with insurance.

This book covers other surgeries available and the requirements for acceptability. These surgeries are top surgery, breast augmentation, and orchiectomies.

Surgeries also require you to complete steps. For most affirming transgender surgeries, there are long waiting lists of up to 2.5 years. To get on their wait list it may cost up to $5,000 or more.

A small percentage of transgender people get GCS to complete their transition. The relief from gender dysphoria post-surgery is well worth it.

Note: GCS is gender confirmation surgery. They also call this bottom surgery within the transgender community. This is when they transform the genitals.

Some WPATH requirements are consistent through all the surgeries. There are several surgeries performed for gender confirmation surgery.

What are those requirements? Some surgeons who perform GCS provide their requirements on their website. WPATH supplies guidelines to follow. Those guidelines are what I will give you here. There are more surgeons performing GCS all the time, so make sure you check for someone close to you.

WPATH's requirements are:

•—Breast/chest and genital surgeries need the patient to have documentation of persistent gender dysphoria. They need a qualified mental health professional to document it.

•—Some surgeons need medical clearance from your primary care doctor and others. You need to have the mental strength in making this decision. You also need to have the mental fortitude to go through the surgery and recovery.

•—Some surgeons may need a current HIV test, whether positive or negative. This applies to transgender females.

Some surgeries have added criteria. This includes preparation and treatment comprising feminizing/masculinizing hormone therapy. Also, one year of continuous living in a gender role congruent with their gender identity. Persistent gender dysphoria may no longer be a roadblock. Some transgender individuals may not have gender dysphoria but still, want surgeries.

•—**Mastectomy and creation of a male chest for transgender males:**

　†—Persistent, well-documented gender dysphoria;

　†—Capability to make an informed decision and to consent for treatment;

　†—Legal age in the country in which the patient gains surgery;

　†—Control of significant mental or medical health concerns. They do not need prior hormone therapy.

•—**Breast augmentation (implants/lipo filling) transgender females:**

　†—Persistent, well-documented gender dysphoria;

　†—Capability to make an informed decision and to consent for treatment;

　†—Legal age in the country in which the patient gets surgery;

　†—Control of significant mental or medical health concerns. They do not need prior hormone therapy.

Note: Not required but transgender female patients should wait for breast augmentation at least one year on hormones. The purpose is to allow the breasts to form and grow on hormones to get more esthetic results. Also, the tissue between the breasts can lift causing problems.

•—Requirements for genital surgery (two referrals). These requirements are specific to the surgery needed.

•—**The following requirements are for hysterectomies and ovariectomies for a transgender male. Also, orchiectomies for transgender females:**

　†—Persistent, well-documented gender dysphoria;

　†—Ability to make an informed decision and to consent for treatment;

　†—Legal age in the country in which the patient gets surgery;

†—Control of significant mental or medical health concerns. They do not need prior hormone therapy.

†—Twelve continuous months on hormone therapy proper for the patient's goals. This is unless the patient has a medical condition preventing taking hormones. Also, if they are unwilling to take hormones.

•—**Requirements for metoidioplasty or phalloplasty for transgender males. Also, vaginoplasty for transgender females:**

†—Persistent, well-documented gender dysphoria;

†—Ability to make an informed decision and to consent for treatment;

†—Legal age in the country in which the patient gets surgery;

†—Control of significant mental or medical health concerns. They do not need prior hormone therapy.

†—Twelve continuous months on hormone therapy proper for the patient's goals. This is unless the patient has a medical condition which prevents taking hormones. Also, if they cannot take hormones or are unwilling.

†—Twelve continuous months living in the gender congruent with their gender identity;

Post-surgery the patient should have regular visits for up to a year with mental health or medical professionals. These restrictions are to ensure the patient is ready and positive they want these surgeries.

CHAPTER FOUR: AFFIRMATION – LEGAL NAME AND GENDER CHANGE

"There will be haters, there will be doubters, there will be non-believers, then there will be you, proving them wrong."
—Anonymous

Changing your identification to your authentic self is affirming. This process varies from state to state. It can also vary county by county within a state. It is best to check ahead of time. Get this done so your new gender does not conflict with your ID picture.

Changing ID and birth certificates in some states will require affirming surgery. Other states need a letter from a medical person confirming you have transitioned. With the letter, some may also need a court order that changed your name/gender in the state you are living in.

There are states requiring you to have been expressing as your new gender for at least one year. Ensure you check requirements for your state. Some transgender advocacy groups have pages set up for all 50 states.

CHAPTER FIVE: WHY DO I STILL HAVE GENDER DYSPHORIA POST TRANSITION?

"Growth is painful. Change is painful. But nothing is as painful as staying stuck somewhere you don't belong."
—Mandy Hale

For many in the transgender community, they may find their gender dysphoria remains. Transitioning, even if partial, will relieve the gender dysphoria to livable levels.

Before transitioning when a transgender person looks in a mirror, they will not see the person they know they are. As the hormones work, they may see the person they know they are. When this happens, it can be a wonderful experience.

They may also get gender dysphoria by looking in the mirror. Transgender women who still have facial hair may have gender dysphoria. They may also get gender dysphoria if they had laser hair removal, but the white whiskers remain. Having to shave or to touch the whiskers may trigger gender dysphoria.

The most effective thing a person can do to relieve their gender dysphoria is hormones. Hormones produce many changes the transgender person can sense. If their hormone levels are more congruent with their gender, they may feel better and see changes.

CHAPTER SIX: WHEN GENDER DYSPHORIA FORCES YOU TO TRANSITION

"What is worse? Accepting your child's gender identity?
Or burying them because you couldn't?
Refuse to be your child's first bully!!!"
—Anonymous

For some, the gender dysphoria may be so bad they need to transition. This can happen at any age. Older transgender people are finding they cannot relieve their gender dysphoria by cross-dressing.

Being transgender is not a decision we make. It is also not a fad. We are born this way. Gender dysphoria can proceed to the point of contemplating suicide. It is the time for the transgender person to make a hard decision and transition. Though I call it a decision, the only decision is to live or die. To be transgender is not a choice. We are born this way.

If the transgender person has a wife and family, it may be much harder to come out. The transgender person may lose someone in their life they love.

The losses endured may be unavoidable. It can also have a negative effect on their vulnerable mental health. There are organizations and other transgender people you can reach out to help you through the worst of times. Most of the transgender community is a close community, and many will reach out to help you. You only need to ask.

PART SEVEN

Discrimination

CHAPTER ONE: DISCRIMINATION

"Darkness cannot drive out darkness: only light can do
that. Hate cannot drive out hate: only love can do that."
"I have decided to stick to love...Hate is too great a
burden to bear."
—Martin Luther King, Jr.

Discrimination affects most in the transgender community and causes mental health problems. The transgender community is the most oppressed community in the United States. Transgender women of color are more oppressed than the rest of the community.

Discrimination does not just happen. There are steps with discrimination and oppression being the endpoint. Having knowledge of the Cycle of Oppression may help in stopping the cycle. The oppression, repression, stereotypes, etc. must stop before we can end discrimination. This would make the world much better for all. The problem is people think they need to control everyone. This chapter will cover how discrimination progresses. Also, the kinds of discrimination.

Older transgender people know the hateful things that people do and say. Who would sign up for verbal, physical and silent attacks? We go through a transition to feel whole like everyone else.

I want the reader to understand some of the negative treatment transgender people face daily. I hope this does not deter you from transitioning. By transitioning, you will feel the wholeness cisgender people take for granted.

CHAPTER TWO: WHAT IS DISCRIMINATION

"Let's practice motivation and love, not discrimination and hate."
—Zendaya

Discrimination is a dirty, vile, and hurtful behavior. Discrimination is the unjust or prejudicial treatment of people or things. It is an intolerance to those people perceived as different. This can be because of sex, religion, color, ethnicity, and gender identity, among others done to marginalized people.

Though the transgender community has seen advances they still are behind the rights that the LGBQ community has accomplished to recieve. There is a negative atmosphere against the transgender community caused by current political actions. The transgender community has experienced a backward movement by the current administration. I do not want this book to be about political sides. My aim is to remain bi partisan.

Whether they target a single person or a large group for discrimination, it can cause anxiety. There are many ways discrimination occurs. There is a current move to erase transgender people from society by disallowing them the ability to exist. Bathroom bills, religious liberty laws, and redefining what gender is are discrimination.

Attacks on the transgender community can seem daunting. To produce a change for the community, we need many allies. People who have a loved one or fellow worker who is transgender can see we are a human with love, feelings, and talents like everyone else.

I will expand more on some of the above topics, so you have insight before coming out. There are many ways and many things people may do to discriminate. It does not have to be verbal. There is body language, staring, and face manipulation. These are harmful when faced daily.

We may consider pictures, the written word, spoken word, non-verbal signals discriminatory. Bigotry is discrimination. And to be clear, bigotry is not in the eyes of the abuser, it is in the eyes of the abused. Bigotry is in the eyes of the attacked.

Different Forms of Discrimination

There are five types of discrimination. Some people may not even know they are discriminating against someone. Though, the person discriminating against someone knows what they are doing. It is a way to lower a person's worth, self-esteem, and be hurtful.

There are many marginalized groups discriminated against. Discrimination, hate, fear start when a person or group differs from the main society. It may be religious. They may think only their religion is right. So, they discriminate against people, not of their religion. It may be sex, gender, disabilities, affectional orientation, ethnicity, color, country of origin, gender identity, and others

Direct Discrimination

This discrimination is the easiest to detect. Direct discrimination happens when a person is treated negatively. This may be because of specific characteristics or perceived characteristics. Their association with a marginalized person may also be a motive for discrimination.

Example: A cake shop will not make a cake because you are transgender, or a bar owner refuses to serve you because you are transgender.

Direct discrimination is the most hurtful form of discrimination. This is because the perpetrator aims it right at the person or group with the specific characteristic.

Indirect Discrimination

This is when organizations, schools or governments pass rules or laws which they enforce in a uniform matter, but they write them in a way to affect a group with specific characteristics. This discrimination is much harder to prove. They may pass these rules, policies, or laws saying health or safety concerns. They justify bathroom laws claiming safety concerns of females because of transgender women using the bathrooms. We discuss more about the bathroom laws in another part of this book.

Associative Discrimination

This is when a person discriminates against another because of their relationship to the person with protected characteristics.

Perceptive Discrimination

When a person discriminates against another because of the perceived protected characteristics.

Harassment

Harassment is when someone attacks a person with protected characteristics through spoken words, gestures, written words, images, and jokes.

Subtle Discrimination

Subtle discrimination is when a person may drawback or treat them differently because the person has specific characteristics. They may not even know they are doing it or realize this is discrimination.

More on Discrimination

• – Two-thirds of those experiencing a hate crime or incident did not report it to anyone.

• – Fewer than one in 10 victims who have reported hate crimes and incidents to the police had it lead to a conviction.

• – Thirty-eight percent of transgender people have experienced physical intimidation and threats. Eighty-one percent have experienced silent harassment. (e.g. being stared at/whispered about). <1>

If harassment and discrimination go on for a length of time, the victim can experience worse depression and physical health effects.

The Cycle of Oppression

Oppression is the abuse of power of a stronger person or group to make a group or person feel less human. It is an unending cycle of unjust treatment of an oppressed group. They can portray oppression in unusual ways. We have seen this by the government rescinding protections for the LGBTQ community. Bathroom bills are oppression. You may find it interesting in how this puts the transgender community in less than the human view.

I provide this information so you have this knowledge. It can help with advocacy. It may help to understand the cycle to know why so many negative stereotypes exist. This can help advocates in understanding to stop the cycle with advocacy.

First Step: Differences

Our society expects everyone to live within an unwritten set of social rules. These rules can be about anything or anyone. It is the cis-normative rule where there are only two genders. (Cis-normative: the belief there is only male and female genders). This is far from true, but society would like us to believe everyone fits into only two boxes. When filling out forms, they have only male or female check boxes. There are only male or female bathrooms. Male or female clothes. There are too many instances to list.

When you do not follow these social beliefs (rules), people consider you different. They relate these differences to all who are a part of the specific class or group. For years, the stereotype where all gay and transgender people are pedophiles has existed. And it still does. Most pedophiles are cisgender white males. The stereotype of transgender women as men in dresses exists to this day. If we educate people about who we are, and why we transition, then stereotypes fall out of existence. Education is not a fix-all solution, but it is a good start.

Second Step: Stereotypes

As mentioned in the differences, these differences become stereotypes. They then associate those stereotypes to everyone in that specific group. A stereotype is a preconceived or oversimplified generalization about a group of people or identity. These can be positive or negative stereotypes. People learn stereotypes through family, friends, and society. The fault in stereotypes, positive or negative is they are untrue. No one person is like another.

One of the more hurtful stereotypes about transgender people is we have a mental illness and may have confusion. Sorry, I am not and have never had confusion over who I am. The transgender community uses mental health professionals at a higher rate. Many of the reasons for this higher rate is because of the negative treatment of the transgender community endures.

Stereotypes grip marginalized groups and keep the cycle of oppression going. We need to embrace the differences each other has, as this makes the world interesting. If everyone was the same, it would be hard to pick out spouses or friends.

Third Step: Prejudice

Prejudices are preconceived generalizations about a group or identity. Prejudice is a negative or limiting belief about a certain group or identity. One prejudice is all people with HIV+ are gay. This prejudice started because HIV appeared to be a gay disease. We know no it is not but this prejudice still exists. HIV+ has become prejudice against the transgender community because some transgender women have sex with gay men (not true). Remember, gay men do not want to be with a woman.

Some people believe transgender females are gay men dressing up to get other men. This is how the HIV+ stereotype was born for transgender females. Transgender people are all diverse types of affectional orientation. So, this stereotype is also untrue.

Fourth Step: Discrimination

Discrimination is when they direct the prejudices at a targeted group to bring pain. When someone has both the prejudice and the power, they use the power to deny access to or limit someone's ability to receive resources. They may do this through legislation, refusal of service, or not applying equal rights to a targeted group. Discrimination affects people on an individual basis, from one person to another. As said earlier, the transgender community is the most marginalized right now. This may be because of misunderstandings of what being transgender is.

Education, education, education. I cannot say it enough. The only way we can end this cycle is by ensuring people know we are an individual like them. The only difference is we embrace our authenticity. We are not any different than the next person.

Fifth Step: Oppression

So here we are at oppression. This is not the last step in the cycle of oppression. Oppression is discrimination on a society level. It does not accomplish this on a one-on-one basis, but at a larger level. A group with power can oppress another weaker group. States without non-discrimination laws for transgender people are oppressing the community. They are doing this by giving society and businesses the right to discriminate against the transgender community.

When oppressing a community, they can become a target for violence and further discrimination. For other ethnicities besides white in the transgender community, the oppression can end up doubling, or worse. Transgender women of color may find themselves a target more so than transgender white women. The average age for transgender women of color is 35 years old. It is important to produce a change in society. If we do not, we may find the whole transgender community facing the same violence. Besides, these are our fellow sisters in this fight.

Sixth Step: Internalized Oppression

When members of the targeted group, believe the socialized beliefs, they are then experiencing internalized oppression. Society teaches many prejudices and stereotypes about the transgender community from an early age. Therefore, it is easy seeing how internalized oppression may affect the already oppressed.

If we face these beliefs from an early age, they may stick with us into adulthood. These oppressive beliefs may be to blame for why it becomes so hard as a transgender person to come out. For young children who are transgender and come out, they may not yet have endured the negative side of society. This may be why they find it easier to stand as themselves.

Seventh Step: Stereotypes Redone

Stereotypes redone is when a person or a group does not attempt something because they have heard all their life transgender people cannot do it. An example is when a transgender person does not get a job because they are transgender. The next generation comes along and hears this stereotype and may have the belief they are not employable.

The Cycle Starts Over

You can see how this cycle continues. See the diagram below on how this cycle runs, and how each step feeds into the next. People use oppression to control groups of people. It may be a dictator using oppression to gain control and keep it.

<1> Stonewall. (n.d.). Retrieved from LGBT Facts and Figures: http://www.stonewall.org.uk/media/lgbt-facts-and-figures

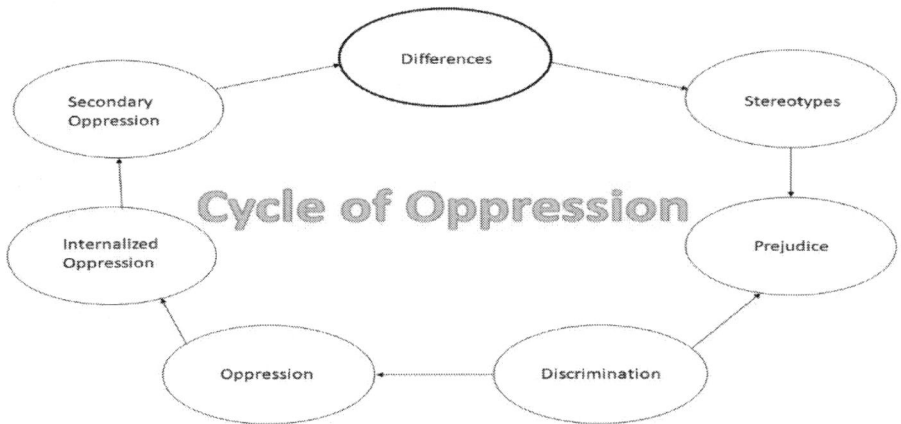

Differences

Secondary Oppression

Stereotypes

Cycle of Oppression

Internalized Oppression

Prejudice

Oppression

Discrimination

CHAPTER THREE: LOOKS, STARES, POINTING, AND LAUGHS. THEY HURT!

"I'd rather have a fake smile, than a nasty stare."
—Tamara Ecclestone

The most consistent form of discrimination may come from non-verbal abuse. The consistency of non-verbal discrimination can become the most harmful to their mental health. Continued bullying, harassment, and discrimination can cause trauma.

Many people discriminate through non-verbal techniques. They may point, look, stare, etc. Some may not realize how rude and hurtful this is. This reaction may be because of the fear of the unknown. If the media and society continue to perpetuate the stereotypes, oppression continues. The public needs to know to stare, pointing, laughing, etc. are hurtful.

Once people meet a transgender person, they may wonder why they ever feared us to begin with. Most transgender people convey love. They are also protective of other transgender people.

Because a transgender person may normalize non-verbal signals, it is still hurtful and negative to their mental health. You may find yourself hurt by someone, but let no one see it. With no response from you about their hate, they may not continue their hurtful quest. I know it may be hard but try not to give them satisfaction.

For some transgender people who come out, they may decide their calling is advocating for the community. By being an advocate, you can help affect the change the community needs. What you do now may have a positive impact on the future. The bonus is it may relieve the depression you have

I try to ignore those who wish to judge me through their stares. I wish they would remember their parents teaching them staring is impolite.

CHAPTER FOUR: NON-DISCRIMINATION LAWS

"It is not our differences that divide us. It is our inability to recognize, accept, and celebrate those differences."

Many people believe the LGBQ and transgender communities are asking for special rights. Our goal is to achieve equal rights. People do not realize it is not illegal to discriminate against transgender people. There are no protections for jobs, housing, or public accommodation.

Some states have non-discrimination laws for affectional orientation but not for gender identity. There may be many reasons for this. They may have had their law in place for a while and not updated it. They may have tried to update their law and had opposition.

Nineteen states and D.C. have full non-discrimination laws for the LGBTQ community. They are; California, Colorado, Connecticut, Delaware, Hawaii, Illinois, Iowa, Maine, Maryland, Massachusetts, Minnesota, Nevada, New Hampshire, New Jersey, New Mexico, Oregon, Rhode Island, Vermont, Washington, and the District of Columbia.

Utah has a non-discrimination law for the whole LGBTQ community but does not protect public accommodation. (public accommodation is using public services)

New York and Wisconsin have a non-discrimination law which only covers affectional orientation. They do not accommodate protection for the transgender community.

The following 28 states have no protections for the whole LGBTQ community: Alabama, Alaska, Arizona, Arkansas, Florida, Georgia, Idaho, Indiana, Kansas, Kentucky, Louisiana, Michigan, Mississippi, Missouri, Montana, Nebraska, North Carolina, North Dakota, Ohio, Oklahoma, Pennsylvania, South Carolina, South Dakota, Tennessee, Texas, Virginia, West Virginia, and Wyoming.

Non-discrimination laws do not cover over half the United States for the transgender community. Some transgender people move to states where they find it easier to exist. This does not mean there will not be problems. It means the harassment may be less in those states.

CHAPTER FIVE: REDEFINING GENDER

"All human beings deserve equal treatment, no matter
their gender identity or sexuality."
—Andreja Pejic

The current administration is looking to put in place a new policy redefining gender. This would erase transgender people. This has been the Family Research Council's (FRC) mission for years. The FRC has a five-step program to make it hard for transgender people to exist in society. This is one step of their plan. Bathroom bills and restricting transgender people from the armed services are others.

The Southern Poverty Law Center (SPLC) considers the FRC a hate group. Tony Perkins, who runs the FRC is an Evangelical. He is also President Trump's number one religious' consultant. The Evangelical community funds the FRC. Connecting the dots gets easy when you see the familiarities. These are all current facts.

Thus, it is important to be out, be proud, and be active in the transgender community. A few people want to end the LGBTQ community's existence. These few people have a loud voice in politics right now. What the community can do towards acceptance will help future transgender people to exist in society. That time will come soon. (I hope!!!)

By redefining gender, it may reduce the ability of the transgender community to receive public services. Transgender people can receive affirming medical interventions to become more congruent with their gender. The ability to receive these services may dissolve if they redefine gender.

CHAPTER SIX: EFFECT BATHROOM BILLS HAVE

"bathroom: (n.) where Americans go to argue about gender while the country goes down the toilet."
–Sol Luckman, The Angel's Dictionary

Legislature's pass bathroom bills (including locker rooms) in some states to limit the bathroom people use. This restriction applies to their sex at birth. This limits the ability for transgender people to use bathrooms which reflect their gender identity. These bills only affect public accommodations. This includes public schools, government buildings, among others.

Bathroom laws can hinder transgender school children's ability to stay in school. Many transgender students have problems with using the restroom. The government need not make it harder to stay in school. Some schools require transgender students to use the nurse's restroom. This is a hardship. Some transgender people, including students, end up holding their urine in search of a friendly restroom. This can have negative effects including bladder infections and kidney damage. When transgender students attend high school, they can find it unbearable to continue. They may drop out of school.

Those who say this is not discrimination need to recheck definitions. Bathroom bills protect no one. In fact, it puts females at a greater risk of assault.

By passing these bills, it puts transgender women at a far greater risk of violence when using the men's restroom.

Many transgender men on hormones grow beards. They look like men after being on hormones for a while. This means you have transgender men with beards using the women's restroom. This is scary for transgender males and women. The original problem becomes moot because now cisgender men can walk into the women's restroom saying they are a transgender male.

No law will stop a person from assaulting someone. They are already breaking a law by assaulting the person.

The transgender person embodies their identified gender. If they are transgender, they live their identified gender daily and are not a male one day and a female the next day. Their transition is a commitment to their identity.

CHAPTER SEVEN: VIOLENCE IN THE TRANSGENDER COMMUNITY

"So much time lost, so much of my childhood gone, because nobody ever asked the right questions."
—April Daniels, Dreadnought

For many cisgender people, they do not know about the transgender community including the violence and hate endured daily. If they knew the facts about the transgender community, more would care about their existence. People would find some of the facts about the transgender community astounding.

The fear and hatred of the transgender community cause violence. There are men who see transgender women as a fetish. They consider it to be gay sex. They do not want their friends to find out, so they murder the transgender women after having sex with them. Many people do not understand who we are. This causes the fear, hate, violence cycle to run. By oppressing people, it makes it easier for society to treat them as a "lower class." By seeing transgender people as less than human, it makes it easier to discriminate and be violent against them. The stigmas and prejudices promoted about transgender people are untrue. Transgender people are human like anyone else.

Year over year the number of transgender people killed becomes a record. In 2017 there were at least 28 transgender murders. The majority were transgender women of color. I say at least 28 murders because there are transgender people murdered may not be identified as transgender. There are many reasons for not identifying their loved one as transgender. The most used excuse is embarrassment and religious beliefs.

Twenty-eight murders may not seem like many. Remember that the transgender community is only 0.6 percent or 1.4 million people in the United States. This number equates to the highest murder rate in the U.S. Most of those murdered are transgender women of color. If you count 25 of the 28 murders as transgender women of color, the rate ends up being 15.3/100,000 murders of transgender women of color. Though this number is high, it may be higher. This number is three times higher than the population in whole.

The family may not identify their transgender family member after suicide. It may be because the family is religious and does not believe in the transgender community. It may also be an embarrassment. Whatever the reason, they are disrespecting and disowning their family member.

CHAPTER EIGHT: FRIENDS AND LOVED ONE'S DON'T REALIZE THEY ARE TRANSPHOBIC.

"Closets kill. They suffocate us. We drown in the refuse of our own lies, lies that say we're alright. We're only alright when we can be seen for who we are."
—David Husted

L oved one's may not realize when they are being transphobic. There are things they can say without realizing they may be hurtful to their transgender loved one.

Though it may be harmful to the transgender person to endure this, it may be a wonderful time for learning. If the transgender person does not correct someone, they may not know what they are doing is hurtful.

So, what is hurtful? The following list gives you some examples:

• – If you are out in public and meet someone you know, but your transgender friend does not, do not introduce them as your transgender friend, child, or loved one. This is outing them for no reason.
• – Do not use or supply a transgender person's dead name (the previous name before transition). It is a dead name for a reason.
• – Do not use the wrong pronouns. It is understandable to use the wrong ones by accident if you knew the old gender for a while.
• – Do not out a person for any other reason. This is their journey and their right to come out as needed. It may also be harmful to tell the wrong person.

It is OK to not understand what transgender is. To understand what your loved one is going through it may help to get a general understanding of what it is.

If they even think it may be hurtful, they should discuss it with the transgender person. Or educate themselves on the transgender community. Transgender people do not aim to be difficult. There are many nuances involved in transgender life's and how the transgender community lives.

PART EIGHT

Suicide. The Reasons and Facts

CHAPTER ONE: THE TRANSGENDER COMMUNITY AND SUICIDE

"The only way I will rest in peace is if one day transgender people aren't treated the way I was, they're treated like humans, with valid feelings and human rights. Gender needs to be taught about in schools, the earlier the better. My death needs to mean something."
—LEELAH ALCORN

This is not an entertaining subject to write about. I pondered whether to have a section on suicide. The data on suicide attempts for the transgender community is one of the highest in the country. Some individuals consider the transgender community a deranged and mentally ill community. They claim we have mental health issues. In this section, I illustrate why the transgender community has a larger rate of mental health care usage. I also give a few factors.

The hate, words, gawking, pointing, and laughing diminish a transgender person's ability to exist. I hope that society will realize that their hateful acts hurt and kill. I would hope that society thinks twice before acting hatefully. If anybody has ever said to you words do not harm, inform them words hurt. Words kill.

As reiterated earlier, if you feel suicidal and plot to take your life, talk to someone. Call a suicide hotline or communicate to an acquaintance. Your time on this earth is worth it, and we love you. The last section of this book has references, including the Transgender Lifeline. Transgender people staff the hotline. This allows communication with a human being who may know what you are going through.

Trans Lifeline: US: 877-565-8860 Canada: 877-330-6366

CHAPTER TWO: MARGINALIZATION OF THE TRANSGENDER COMMUNITY

"Being told you are not who you know yourself to be is
trauma [page 321]"
—Elijah C. Nealy, Transgender Children and Youth:
Cultivating Pride and Joy with Families in Transition

The transgender community at present is the most marginalized in the United States. It is the most marginalized in many countries around the world. There are smaller parts of the transgender community which experience higher marginalization. Transgender women of color are the most marginalized. A transgender woman of color experiences an average life of 35 years. For those over 35 who are viewing this I would relate to you I am overjoyed you are still with us. Scary.

Nobody would make a choice to be born transgender. A transgender person will experience bitter, and violent individuals. Being our authentic selves is worth the risk we withstand. Walking around in a world where you are acting your birth sex can be painful. It can take its toll on an individual. Though coming out for anybody can be painful, the transgender community faces more after coming out.

There are prejudice and stigmas producing a detrimental and vicious tone. Some of these prejudices are the same the rest of the LGBTQ communities face. These stigmas and prejudices are not correct. For many, these untruths continue because they do not desire the truth about transgender individuals.

The dread of the unknown influences how individuals recognize the transgender community. That dread can spiral into hate, hate into violence. It is essential to educate whoever we can. Challenge the stigmas and prejudices when you face them. Explain to others why they are false.

Bathroom bills show us how misinformation can have a powerful effect on an individual's life. Some individuals will not accept the facts about this because they may have a sealed mind and assume they are right. This needs to evolve.

The transgender community is 0.6 percent of the U.S. populace. This is negligible. There are groups of individuals who maintain the laws should not change for such a limited group. What if their child, grandchild, or other loved one comes out as transgender? Are they going to shift their mind? Should we not get equal rights?

All the negativity towards the transgender community is part of why we find ourselves marginalized. We deal with such a tremendous rate of suicide attempts.

The transgender community has a day set aside to recognize those we have lost to homicide over the preceding year. Some remember those who took their own life. These numbers continue to rise every year. The statistics supplied later in this section illustrate these statistics are at epidemic levels. If these figures existed in the cisgender community, they would already have laws in place to lower them.

Marginalization, oppression, prejudice, stigma, bigotry. All those terms have hate and violence associated with them. Society can improve. Why is religion so powerful in the world, but violence against oppressed people continues? Religions should not preach hate and oppression. Everyone is equal in God's eyes.

There is an expression "Love the sinner, hate the sin." This expression, even though it may appear nice enough can become hateful. Jesus never stated this. He never taught about hate. It is "Love thy neighbor as thyself." It is not "Love thy neighbor but hates their sin." Judgment is for God. This expression has other issues. It can become hard to veer from the hate part. Changing someone else's sin is not another person's responsibility. It is not their duty to pass judgment either. This expression is likewise a construct of oppression. It can change to a vicious statement and most LGBTQ people criticize the expression. Everyone sins. No one is without sin.

There is an abundance of effort going forward to shape people's minds and societies views. To sponsor change, it may require changing one person at a time. Let us do our part.

Because you are a part of a marginalized community does not imply you cannot be proud of who you are. Walk out the door with your head carried high. You are you, and there is nobody more magnificent.

CHAPTER THREE: CAUSES OF SUICIDE ATTEMPTS

"Everybody goes through difficult times, but it is those who push through those difficult times who will eventually become successful in life. Don't give up, because this too shall pass."
—Jeanette Coron

Some of the points in this chapter are painful to address because I have encountered them. The agony of one individual is education for others. I realize people will evolve. Life will become easier for transgender individuals. We see it with the affirming younger generations.

Many things lead to someone feeling their life will not get better. For a transgender person, it may be the many years they had to pretend to be a person they were not. Some transgender individuals have developed depression from years in the wrong body.

I cannot provide a complete list of what may prompt someone to take their life. I will illustrate what a transgender person faces which can create distress. Being transgender does not create it. It is because our identity is diverse from civilization's unwritten rules. Being transgender comes with despair, loss, and struggles to live in a culture which views gender as binary.

The National Center for Transgender Equality (NCTE) carried out an online survey. They call it the 2015 United States Transgender Survey (USTS). This survey asks many questions about the hazards and roadblocks to being transgender. This includes depression and suicide attempts.

The survey revealed the suicide attempt rate is the same as in past studies of suicide in the transgender community. The rate for transgender adults is 41 percent. <1> Out of 1.4 million individuals (0.6 percent of the populace), <2> 574,000 have tried suicide at least one time in their life. The whole LGBTQ community experiences a rate of 10 to 20 percent. <3> These figures are unacceptable, and we need to fight to lower them. Education is our strongest weapon. One loss of life is one too many. These figures do not comprise those who officials and families identify as the incorrect gender. This includes misgendering by families, authorities, and others. The amount is apt to be higher.

This data presents a further perspective on why there is a mental health crisis in the transgender community. For transgender individuals, desperation can be a killer.

Cisgender people feel relaxed in their body. The transgender person feels incongruent with their body (pre-transition) causing anxiety and depression. This depression can intensify to suicidal thought, or worse. If they think they will never be their authentic self, they may conclude they would be better off taking their life. The only thing permanent is death. Any situation a minor or adult is in will change in time. The belief that suicide is the relief to their plight is appalling. Many in the community pray they will wake up as their authentic self. As we grow older, our prayers may focus around preferring not to wake up the next morning.

By taking their life they will never be their authentic self. There are many negative factors about being transgender. This can cause it to be harder to realize the wonderful part of being you. Suicide revolves around most of the negative things we discuss in this book.

Parents, spouses, and acquaintances, among others, thrust their negativity on the transgender person. It might be the discrimination they have to live with. They may live on the streets because they are not employable. This can lead to secondary oppression.

The reasons are infinite, but not permanent. I live with severe major depressive disorder every day. When someone stares, laughs, etc. I would prefer to show it does not hurt me. However, it hurts. I overlook it when possible. Sometimes it is so blatant it is tough to overlook. This can lead to my depression getting worse. I seek to find something to keep my mind busy, so the dark thoughts succeed some. What you have no control over should not get the best of you. It took more than eight years with my current counselor to beat this into my head.

What troubles you the most may not matter much. If your mood is down, it may not take a considerable spark to put an individual in the blackness of depression. When one door closes, another opens. For those with existing depression, you may have heard this. I know I have. I became tired of hearing it. But every time I heard it, it carried me closer to where I am now. Though I realize my depression will never disappear, I have a better command of it now.

This book and forthcoming books of mine are one of the best means for me to give back and to deal with my depression better. If I do not, I may end up back where I was five or six years ago. I was sleeping 16 hours a day. This I do not want again. I felt lifeless. Lonely. Alone. When I look back, I cannot figure out how I am here now.

I can say it becomes better. My life will never be what it was before my depression, but I would not be the individual I am now. My life feels more purposeful now. I suffer daily with my depression. Giving back makes my life worthwhile.

Remember this, it becomes better. Even if the depression remains, you can knock it down by finding something pleasurable to do and good people to do it with. Giving back by advocacy is a heart-lifting way to treat your depression. If you take your life you will never see who you may have been.

<1> – The Report of the 2015 US Transgender Survey, James, S. E., Herman, J. L., Rankin, S., Keisling, M., Mottet, L., & Anafi, M. (2016). The Report of the 2015 U.S. Transgender Survey. Washington, DC: National Center for Transgender Equality., Published in 2016.
<2> – Hoffman, J. (2016, June 30). *Transgender population.* Retrieved from New York Times: https://www.nytimes.com/2016/07/01/health/transgender-population.html
<3> – Ann P. Haas, P. P. (2014). Suicide Attempts among Transgender and Gender Non-conforming Adults.

CHAPTER FOUR: MENTAL HEALTH USAGE RATE FOR THE TRANSGENDER COMMUNITY

"I don't think we should be discriminating against anyone. Transgender people are people and they deserve the best we can give them."
—Orrin Hatch

The transgender community has one of the highest usages of mental health care in the country. There are many sources of this. Gender dysphoria affects an abundant piece of the transgender community. Gender dysphoria alone can lead to an individual having suicidal intentions and seeking to take their own life. The oppression, stigmas, and stereotypes may likewise contribute. For many, harassment happens rather often, sometimes daily.

The general population's usage of mental health care is 6.7 percent. Eighteen percent of the public have an anxiety disorder. For the transgender community, the amount of usage is near 50 percent. <1>

What are the dominating sources? Stigma, exclusion, hatred, and abuse. Dealing with discrimination leaves an individual in a magnified state of caution. When you sense you may encounter prejudice or violence, it may lead to stress and distress.

The many losses of loved ones can influence depression requiring more mental health care.

When an individual thinks they cannot come out, they may seek mental health care. Continued harassment, prejudice, and other factors may give individuals trauma. Some in the community have major depressive disorder precipitated by years of living in the wrong body. Any bullying from oppression can further depression.

It may link the transgender community's mental health usage to the appraisals for discrete steps of transitioning. Some steps of transitioning need letters from mental health professionals.

Some may find it hopeless to get employment because of legal discrimination. This can place them in a perceived lower class. There is class discrimination which affects segments of the community.

HIV is at epidemic levels in the transgender women's community. HIV itself can produce stress and anxiety. Then you add the discrimination HIV+ transgender people encounter.

Transgender individuals outlook and mental health will be better with acceptance. A transgender child loved by their family and cared for in an adequate matter at school have improved grades. The transgender student dropout rate also drops.

For some individuals in the community, they may discover they are lonely. In less populated areas there may not be many like-minded individuals to talk to and provide support. It can likewise be hard to meet friends accepting of transgender individuals.

I will leave you with this. The cisgender community should know what transgender is and accept transgender people for who we are. This will encourage change for the future of 1.4 million people. And these are fellow humans.

<1> - https://www.psychologytoday.com/us/blog/the-truth-about-exercise-addiction/201612/why-transgender-people-experience-more-mental-health, By Katherine Schreiber, Why Transgender People Experience More Mental Health Issues

CHAPTER FIVE: WORDS! THE GOOD, THE BAD, AND THE UGLY

"It hurts when I'm told by my mom tells that most trans people know their gender at a young age. I feel like she is trying to invalidate me. I know I am older, but I am not 'most' trans people."
—Anonymous

W ords hurt. Words kill. There are appropriate words and phrases, and words and phrases which are demeaning. Family and acquaintances should learn

Unacceptable words	Acceptable words
Tranny, shemale, chick with a d---	Trans, transgender, transsexual
Do not use their deadname name	Use their selected and correct name
Do not use pronouns for the sex they were born with.	Use preferred pronouns.

these words. Some of these are hateful.

There are alternative words and phrases that can demean the transgender individual. If an individual is unclear of a word or phrase, do not use it or inquire what is adequate. It further serves to figure out what you will say. If you would not ask a cisgender person, do not ask a transgender individual.

It is never OK to use words as a form of belittling an individual. Times change and words enter and leave out of use. If you are a friend or family member stay informed. When I was growing up, queer was offensive. For some individuals it still is. However, the younger generation has taken the word back and are proud of it.

The reference section provides other things individuals should and should not while interacting with transgender individuals.

PART NINE

Caring for Your Transgender Loved One

CHAPTER ONE: THE TRANSGENDER PERSON AND THEIR LOVED ONES

"Just because my path is different
Doesn't mean I'm lost."
—Anonymous

The transgender person may find themselves without support once they come out. Family and friends may no longer wish to be a part of their life. This can have unfortunate repercussions. Give them love and support during this stage. Even loved ones fine with cross-dressing or expressing their gender before coming out. When your new life becomes something more permanent, the loved ones may turn away.

When this loss takes place, it can harm those affected. This can be equal to the death of a loved one. It puts the transgender person at a greater risk of worsening depression or attempting suicide. The other family members or friends suffer too. They may go through more. Family and friends need to recognize their transgender loved one is happy for the first time in a while. Should they throw away their happiness to make certain others stay happy? The loved one is being selfish to respond yes.

This is when the transgender person starts on their journey to authenticity. Their loved ones should welcome this. This might appear selfish. It is about the transgender individual's life and happiness. This is not a compromise.

Families should not tear apart. They do. The transgender individual needs to recognize family is not always blood. Families are born every day where none of the members are blood-related.

CHAPTER TWO: TRANSGENDER AND MARRIED

"My spouse says he is she. This isn't what I thought my life would look like. Can I do this? Do I stay or do I go? What WILL our life look like? Okay, one day at a time and go from there. As it turns out, I CAN do this. I love her too."
—Anonymous. from Relationship Gardening with Shannon

For many married transgender people, they may find their marriage ends up in a flurry after they come out. This is justifiable because their spouse married the former gender.

Spouses can feel cheated because the transgender person possesses an awareness of being transgender before becoming wed. This may be correct, but the transgender person hopes they never have to transition. There is no excuse for not disclosing. Being transgender is a secret most wish they never deal with.

The spouse may wish to get even. They may seek to turn their kids against the transgender spouse. They should meet and talk to a counselor. Try working things out. It is best for those affected. Do not involve your kids. Children can sense tension. They may end up disowning the cisgender spouse for criticizing the transgender spouse.

Try to get through this time with limited collateral damage as achievable. It makes both spouses lives easier to maneuver.

Roles may vary for marriages surviving the transgender person's transition. The transgender person may wish to do the other's routines. This is a time of exploration. Though the transgender person's personality will little, the rest of their life will change.

If the transgender partner is now female, it may take longer to get ready to go out. It is better no to gender any house chores. Go with the movement.

CHAPTER THREE: WHEN A PARENT COMES OUT TO THEIR CHILDREN

"Even when we are confused about someone's gender, and don't have a greater awareness of what it means to be trans, we have a choice to respond with kindness rather than cruelty."
—C. N. Lester

A transgender person with children might find it hard to come out to them. you may find it difficult to explain to your younger child why you are dressing and presenting differently. For the younger child, it may be best to turn your transition into an explanation they can relate to. For older kids, most will understand what you are explaining them. Most kids will welcome you as transgender.

Make certain your school-age children understand others may ridicule and bully them. Think ahead to provide your kids with a plan to deal with any negativity they encounter. If the transgender parent and their children prepare ahead of time, it might make their school life smoother. Report any bullying to administration officials. Stop the bullying before it becomes out of control. If you cannot stop the bullying, remove your child. (This is essential)

Divorces hurt everybody. The negative side of separating because your transgender is your stress, anxiety, and resentment may arise. If you seek therapy, those involved may make it through this. Coming out the other side is essential. If you have someone outside the relationship to listen and talk to can, this can help. Make certain your kids remain as untouched as doable.

CHAPTER FOUR: THE ANGER

"Be yourself, no matter what. Some will adore you and
some will hate everything about you. But who cares? It's
your life. Make the most of it."
—Anonymous

We have examined the anger loved ones can experience. The transgender person may be bitter. This occurs from how family, friends, and the public treat them. Even if a loved one claims they accept you, they may not. This can come out in unhealthy forms.

If spouses and family members have known the transgender person for a long time, they may continue addressing the transgender person by their deadname and old pronouns. This is never OK. If another person hears them using the incorrect pronouns or their deadname, they may assume this to be OK. It is a sign of respect for the person and who they are to use the correct name and pronouns.

When someone they have known for a while, it may take a while to learn their new name and pronouns. Remind them when they error. It can frustrate and take time. There will be occasions when they use the incorrect name or pronouns without recognizing they did. Let them know you understand it happens. The more you correct the cisgender loved ones the clearer it will be for them to comply.

PART TEN

Extra Information

CHAPTER ONE: IMPORTANT INFORMATION

Knowledge is power. Information is liberating. Education
is the premise of progress, in every society, in every
family.
—Kofi Annan

Some information does not fit into other topics. There is a chapter with facts reflecting on why the transgender community needs advocacy. There are many topics involved in a transgender person's transition and life. They are correcting what was not right by changing their outward appearance. The transgender person needs knowledge in what to do for a successful transition.

CHAPTER TWO: DETRANSITIONING (AKA RETRANSITIONING)

"If I had a choice between a pink pill to turn me to a
female or a blue pill to turn to a male, I would always
pick the pink pill. That's who I am."
—Stephania Kanitsch

Detransitioning is when someone has transitioned but ends up transitioning back to the previous sex. They may realize they are not transgender and go back to their previous gender. It is essential to know you are transgender. There may be other reasons for detransitioning.

It could be where they live is dangerous for a transgender person to be out. Their family may not accept. They may not want to break up their family or marriage.

If they lack the means to survive, they may want a place to live.

There are organizations who report copious amounts of transgender people detransitioning. They try to influence the transgender person, parents, or loved ones. There is no truth to these stories.

There has never been a study or survey on detransitioning done with valid data. These organizations use skewed data to scare transgender people from transitioning. They may use the skewed data to dehumanize the transgender community.

Most transgender people coming out realize what is ahead. There is no valid data, and you do not hear of someone who has detransitioned. Do not let them influence you. Live your life how you want. You are beautiful and authentic.

CHAPTER THREE: YOGYAKARTA PRINCIPLES

"I was a girl once. Turns out it was a phase."
—Anonymous

The Yogyakarta Principles is a document covering human rights. These principles cover rights in the areas of sexual orientation and gender identity. It is the outcome of an international meeting of human rights groups in Yogyakarta, Indonesia, in November 2006. They revised the Principle in 2017. In the 2017 revision, they included gender expression and sex characteristics, and several new principles.

The document provides International legal standards against the abuse of human rights of lesbian, gay, bisexual, transgender (LGBT) and intersex people. All signers must abide by these principles of LGBTQ human rights.

This document is important to the LGBTQ community, so I have included it in this book. There are some U.S. people who signed the Principles document. The proceeding is the principles. I am only supplying the title of each principle.

1 — The Right to Universal Enjoyment of Human Rights
2 — The Rights to Equality and Non-Discrimination
3 — The Right to Recognition before the Law
4 — The Right to Life
5 — The Right to Security of the Person
6 — The Right to Privacy
7 — The Right to Freedom from Arbitrary Deprivation of Liberty
8 — The Right to a Fair Trial
9 — The Right to Treatment with Humanity while in Detention
10 — The Right to Freedom from Torture and Cruel, Inhumane, or Degrading Treatment or Punishment
11 — The Right to Protection from all Forms of Exploitation, Sale, and Trafficking of Human Beings
12 — The Right to Work
13 — The Right to Social Security and to Other Social Protection Measures
14 — The Right to an Adequate Standard of Living
15 — The Right to Adequate Housing
16 — The Right to Education

17 — The Right to the Highest Attainable Standard of Health
18 — Protection from Medical Abuses
19 — The Right to Freedom of Opinion and Expression
20 — The Right to Freedom of Peaceful Assembly and Association
21 — The Right to Freedom of Thought, Conscience, and Religion
22 — The Right to Freedom of Movement
23 — The Right to Seek Asylum
24 — The Right to Found a Family
25 — The Right to take part in Public Life
26 — The Right to take part in Cultural Life
27 — The Right to Promote Human Rights
28 — The Right to Effective Remedies and Redress
29 — Accountability

The U.S. does not follow some of these Principles in entirety. Some countries do not follow this document. Until then, we need to keep on fighting for our equality.

CHAPTER FOUR: RAY BLANCHARD'S HARMFUL TRANSGENDER RHETORIC

"Don't hate what you don't understand."
—John Lennon

Ray Blanchard coined the term "autogynephilia". It describes trans women with an erotic desire "to be women." He hypothesized that gender dysphoria experienced by transgender females is of two types; "homosexual" gender dysphoria and "non-homosexual" gender dysphoria. This is not why transgender people transition. First, gay men like men. Second, transgender females could cross-dress if they have a fetish to be a female. Being transgender is not a fad. Coming out and being out can be stressful, hurtful, and loss inflicted. It is much easier to cross-dress. Third, this theory does not explain transgender males.

Blanchard's study is hurtful. Some conservative and religious groups use his research to disavow the transgender community. The Family Research Council and other hate group organizations have used his research. They are hate groups as determined by the Southern Poverty Law Center (SPLC).

These organizations skew valid research to make it fit what they want to preach. One doctor supplied research which other researchers debunked. It stated there was a sizable percentage of post-op transgender people regretted transitioning. There are groups that use this research knowing it is a lie. This helps them to make the transgender community look less than human.

CHAPTER FIVE: COMING OUT AS TRANSGENDER IS NOT A FAD

"People didn't start coming out as transgender after Caitlyn Jenner as a fad. They came out, because she inspired them to be brave enough to be themselves."
—Anonymous

There are people saying that coming out and being transgender is a fad. One problem with this statement. Fads are not dangerous, you do not lose loved ones, and they are not stressful. There is a current movement, in that transgender people see it is safer to come out. So, there is an increase in the amount coming out as transgender.

Even though it is safer, there is still a huge risk of coming out as transgender. Society looks down on the transgender community. They see only two genders, and they believe that your sex at birth is your gender. They do not believe that gender and sex are two different things. Closed minds produce closed hearts. When you open your heart, you open your mind.

Children are coming out younger. This is because they are learning earlier what the difference is. Children have access to information so vast compared to the information available 20 years ago.

If being transgender was a fad, there would not be the hate, harassment, and discrimination. Fads do not push people into taking their life.

Parents of transgender children know it is not a fad. They are losing their son or daughter. This is not how a fad looks. Yes, they are gaining a son or daughter, but for many parents, it is hard to look at it like that. I have no realization of how it feels to be a parent of a trans child. My realization is from how my mom reacted. I know it hurts the parents.

By calling transgender a fad, there is also a new diagnosis. Rapid-Onset Gender Dysphoria (ROGD). [1], [2] This is not a DSM (Diagnostic Statistical Manual of Mental Health Disorders) The people who produced this new diagnosis claim it comes from societal pressure. Please! Anything to justify that transgender people are not real.

They state that most going on this journey are born female-bodied. Their claim is that they are approaching this as if it were an everyday occurrence. I do not think and would hope this is not the truth. There are many transgender people who come out of college. They come out because they are no longer at home and have been able to experience their authentic self. Children in middle and high school experiment with their style or authenticity. But for those unsure of acceptance while still at home, college is a time to explore who you are. It is time to become you.

For parents with a child who has come out as transgender in the recent past, do not feed into this fad belief. This is not what your child is going through. Remember non-binary individuals exist. There are many more children and young adults coming out as transgender non-binary. It might be hard. Accept your child. This makes their life easier. And it keeps your child alive. This is one of many ways to be human.

<1> – https://www.theguardian.com/commentisfree/2018/oct/22/rapid-onset-gender-dysphoria-is-a-poisonous-lie-used-to-discredit-trans-people, Liz Duck-Chong, Sun 21 Oct 2018 15.00 EDT
<2> – https://psychcentral.com/lib/there-is-no-evidence-that-rapid-onset-gender-dysphoria-exists/, There Is No Evidence That Rapid-Onset Gender Dysphoria Exists, By Florence Ashley, B.C.L., LL.B., Last updated: 3 Dec 2018

CHAPTER SIX: TRANSGENDER DISENFRANCHISEMENT IN THE U.S.

"We have to remember that all movements are all connected... Our enemies are the same."
—Gloria Steinem

New voter I.D. laws are restricting tens of thousands of transgender people's voting rights. Why? Because their I.D. may not reflect their gender expression. A report prepared by the Williams Institute revealed that in 2016 there were over 34,000 transgender Americans across eight states that might not vote because of restrictive voter ID laws. <1>

What is in question is for many transgender people, their I.D does not match their appearance? This incongruence in a person's I.D. vs. their expression can make life complicated in other areas. If pulled over by police, they may find their I.D. does not match their looks. It is important that a transgender person change their I.D. as soon as possible. It also outs a person as transgender every time they produce their I.D.

I would add that you ensure you change your gender with your name if possible. They should universalize the process for changing the name and gender on your I.D. This makes it easier from state to state. In some states, you cannot change your gender, even with surgery.

I could change my I.D. and birth certificate. The state where I was born had a recent change in requirements for changing a birth certificate. You no longer need surgery to change your gender on your birth certificate. To change my birth certificate was affirming. It feels good to have the correct name and gender on your I.D.

Make yourself congruent so there is less stress in your life. Your vote needs to count. You count. DO IT!!!

<1> – https://williamsinstitute.law.ucla.edu/research/strict-voter-id-laws-may-disenfranchise-more-than-34000-transgender-voters-in-the-2016-november-election/, Strict Voter ID Laws May Disenfranchise More Than 34,000 Transgender Voters in the 2016 November Election, Jody L. Herman, September 2016

CHAPTER SEVEN: THE DUNNING-KRUGER EFFECT ON THE TRANSGENDER COMMUNITY

"Confidence is the prize given to the mediocre"
—Robert Hughes

This is an interesting subject. Many people do not know what the Dunning-Kruger effect is. I would apply this to most of those who reply on social media that do not understand what being transgender is. <1>

The Dunning-Kruger effect is a cognitive bias in which people of low-ability have unreal superiority and mistake their cognitive ability as greater than it is. This bias of unreal superiority comes from the inability of low-ability people to recognize their lack of ability. This leaves them without the ability to realize their own competence or incompetence.

So how do we apply it to the transgender community? There are people who still believe sex and gender are the same. Science and research are so far beyond that. It does not take much to educate yourself on what transgender is. The more information you have the better equipped you are when talking about issues.

There are also those who only believe in the gender binary and are adamant that our genitals determine our gender. I am not one to get into a discussion unless I am armed with facts. It is rare I join in or reply to comments on social media. Why? No matter how right you are, those with the Dunning-Kruger effect are righter (at least they think they are). Most of us know who and what we are. Having an argument with a person with Dunning-Kruger effect is not winnable.

<1> – https://en.wikipedia.org/wiki/Dunning%E2%80%93Kruger_effect, Dunning–Kruger effect, Wikipedia,

CHAPTER EIGHT: ADVOCACY: THE FACTS SHOW US WHY WE NEED IT

"We are all assigned a gender at birth. Sometimes that assignment doesn't match our inner truth, and there needs to be a new place -- a place for self-identification. I was not born a boy, I was assigned boy at birth. Understanding the difference between the two is crucial to our culture and society moving forward in the way we treat - and talk about - transgender individuals ... In today's globally connected and ever-diversifying world, culture is now more fluid and more flexible than ever -- and so too should be our understanding and perception of gender."
—Geena Rocero

I am supplying facts showing why this is all so important. Some of these facts are in other parts of this book but I wanted to supply them in one central location.

• — There is a higher percentage of transgender people who sign up for the military. Of the 1.4 million transgender people in the U.S., 15,600 serve in the military. <1>

• — Of those who have transitioned, 78 percent of post-transition found comfort with their lives. <2>

• — Gender confirmation surgery (GCS) was first carried out in the U.S. at Johns Hopkins University in 1966. Lili Elbe, a German national, received the first GCS surgery in 1930. <3>

• — To be transgender is not new. Because this is the way we are born, transgender people have been around for a long time. The recorded history of transgender people dates to the Assyrian society in the 25th century B.C. <4>

• — People think we are a threat when using the correct bathrooms. Quite the opposite. Transgender people are at more risk of harm using the restroom of their sex at birth. <5>

• — Transgender people are not gay. Their orientation varies as much as the cisgender community. <6>

• — Transgender people have a higher rate of living below the poverty level. A study found that the transgender person was four times more likely to make less than $10,000 yearly. <7>

• — Twenty-three percent of transgender people have faced discrimination when looking for a home. This research reveals that ten percent of all transgender people interviewed have faced eviction because of their gender identity. <8>

• — Healthcare for transgender people is inadequate in many areas. Many do not have health insurance. They may discriminate others against by their healthcare providers. It is also possible they may not receive care for those things limited to people of certain genders (prostate check, mammogram, and others). There is a 50 percent higher chance of transgender people getting HIV (particularly trans females). <9>

• — The previous DSM had gender identity disorder (GID) as a mental health diagnosis. There are many people who still believe this. DSM V replaced GID with gender dysphoria. This does nothing to quell the critics. Because of our identity, some people think we have confusion in who we are. In our society, it is hard to live a peaceful life if you are different. This situation can lead to more stress, which can lead to higher mental health problems. It also leads to higher physical health problems caused by the depression

• — A high percentage of transgender women of color lose their lives every year by homicide. Why do they lose their life? For nothing. By being themselves. These deaths of transgender people for being themselves is at an epidemic level. Does it make the news? Not much. Year over year the number of homicides in the transgender community breaks records.

• — Ninety-two percent of transgender people attempting suicide did so before age 25. <10>

• — Many older transgender people who are now coming out learned from an early age how to hide their identity and either "man up" or "woman up". This protected us in a society which does not accept us. We have moved forward since then. There are still many negative or unsure feelings about the transgender community.

• — In the United States, 0.6 percent of the adult population (1.4 million people) identify as transgender. <11>

• — Transgender kids and teenagers experience elevated levels of bullying and violence at school. <12>

• — Anti-LGBT violence affects transgender people at an elevated rate.

• — Transgender people are subject to higher rates of police violence. <13>

• — A recent report found that transgender people are 3.7 times more likely to experience police violence than cisgender survivors and victims of anti-LGBT violence (LGBQ). <13>

• — This risk is higher for trans females. They are four times more likely than others to have experienced police violence. <13>

• — Transgender people experience high rates of harassment and discrimination in the workplace.

• — Transgender people face higher-than-average rates of housing discrimination and homelessness. <14>
• — Transgender people find themselves homeless at a rate twice the national average. <14>
• — They are less than half as likely to own their own home than the average American. <14>
• — Nineteen percent of transgender people say someone refused them housing. <14>
• — They evicted Eleven percent for being transgender. <14>

This leaves them more vulnerable to more violence and less able to report it.

Transgender youth

• — In homes of gender-expansive youth, they face a 78 percent chance of negative overtones about the LGBTQ community before coming out. <15>
• — Transgender youth are over two times as likely to face taunting or mocked by family members for their identity than cisgender LGBQ youth. <15>
• — Fifty-one percent of transgender youth never use restrooms or locker rooms matching their gender identity. This may be because the school district they are in does not allow it. <16>
• — Thirty-one percent express themselves in a way that reflects their gender identity in school. <16>
• — In school one in three transgender students may be addressed by their true name. <16>
• — In school one in five transgender students may be addressed by the correct pronouns. <16>
• — Less than a quarter of transgender youth feel they can be themselves at home. <16>
• — Seventy-seven percent of transgender youth have received unwanted sexual comments, jokes, and gestures. <16>
• — Only 16 percent of transgender youth always feel safe at school. <17>
• — Fifty percent of transgender youth have received physical threats because of their identity. <18>
• — Fifty-one percent of transgender youth do not use restrooms at school that aligns with their gender identity. <19>
• — Only 36 percent of all transgender youths' parents get involved with the larger LGBTQ community. <15>
• — For 95 percent of transgender youth, they have trouble sleeping at night. <20>

- — Eighty-five percent of transgender youth and 82 percent of LGBQ rate their stress on a scale of one to ten at a five. <20>
- — About 41 percent of LGBTQ youth received psychological or emotional counseling in the last year. <15>
- — Seventy-three percent of LGBTQ youth have had an experience of verbal threats because of their actual or perceived LGBTQ identity. <15>
- — Only 26% of LGBTQ youth feel safe in the classroom. <15>
- — Seventy-three percent of LGBTQ youth have experienced verbal threats because of their actual or perceived LGBTQ identity. <15>

<1> — https://transequality.org/issues/military-veterans, National Center for Transgender Equality, Issues/Military Veterans

<2> — https://ct.counseling.org/2017/08/counseling-transgender-persons-families/, Counseling Today, Counseling transgender persons and their families By Al Carlozzi August 1, 2017

<3> — https://en.wikipedia.org/wiki/Sex_reassignment_surgery_(male-to-female), Wikipedia, Sex reassignment surgery (male-to-female)

<4> — https://en.wikipedia.org/wiki/Transgender_history, Wikipedia, Transgender History

<5> — https://www.npr.org/2016/05/15/477954537/when-a-transgender-person-uses-a-public-bathroom-who-is-at-risk, NPR, Jeff Brady, May 15, 2016, 7:48 AM ET

<6> — https://www.vox.com/cards/transgender-myths-fiction-facts/sexual-orientation-gender-identity-myth, Vox, Transgender people: 10 common myths, Edited by German Lopez

<7> — https://williamsinstitute.law.ucla.edu/williams-in-the-news/beyond-stereotypes-poverty-in-the-lgbt-community/, Williams Institute, Beyond Stereotypes: Poverty in the LGBT Community, Brad Sears, and Lee Badgett, Published by TIDES | Momentum Issues 4, June 2012

<8> — https://thinkprogress.org/trans-housing-discrimination-study-889129c40c1b/, Think Progress, Housing discrimination against transgender people is even worse than we thought, Zack Ford, April 3, 2017, 7:43 PM

<9> — https://www.hrc.org/resources/understanding-the-transgender-community, Human Rights Campaign, Understanding the Transgender Community

<10> — https://www.thetrevorproject.org/resources/preventing-suicide/facts-about-suicide/#sm.0000amzmpojkxddy10upas5d7rtfw, The Trevor Project, Preventing Suicide: Facts About Suicide

<11> — https://en.m.wikipedia.org/wiki/LGBT_demographics_of_the_United_States, Wikipedia, LGBT Demographics of the United States

<12> — https://www.stopbullying.gov/blog/2016/10/17/school-bullying-and-lesbian-gay-and-bisexual-high-school-students.html, Stop Bullying Dot Gov, School Bullying and Lesbian, Gay, Bisexual, and Transgender Students, Oct 17, 2016, Lisa C. Barrios, Research Application and Evaluation Branch Chief, Division of Adolescent and School Health, Centers for Disease Control and Prevention

<13> — https://transequality.org/sites/default/files/docs/usts/USTS-Full-Report-Dec17.pdf, The Report of the 2015 U.S. Transgender Survey, Chapter 14, James, S. E., Herman, J. L., Rankin, S., Keisling, M., Mottet, L., & Anafi, M. (2016). The Report of the 2015 U.S. Transgender Survey. Washington, DC: National Center for Transgender Equality

<14> — https://transequality.org/sites/default/files/docs/usts/USTS-Full-Report-Dec17.pdf, The Report of the 2015 U.S. Transgender Survey, Chapter 13, James, S. E., Herman, J. L., Rankin, S., Keisling, M., Mottet, L., & Anafi, M. (2016). The Report of the 2015 U.S. Transgender Survey. Washington, DC: National Center for Transgender Equality

<15> — https://assets2.hrc.org/files/assets/resources/2018-YouthReport-NoVid.pdf?_ga=2.27771068.1880459182.1550096788-1042517524.1532103907, Human Rights Campaign, 2018 LGBTQ Youth Report, The Importance of Family

<16> — https://assets2.hrc.org/files/assets/resources/2018-YouthReport-NoVid.pdf?_ga=2.27771068.1880459182.1550096788-1042517524.1532103907, Human Rights Campaign, 2018 LGBTQ Youth Report, Trans Youth Need Our Support

<17> — https://www.out.com/news-opinion/2018/11/16/hrc-publishes-new-data-detailing-how-unsafe-trans-teens-feel-school, Out Dot Com, HRC Publishes New Data Detailing How Unsafe Trans Teens Feel at School, Rose Dommu, November 16, 2018, 10:01 AM EST

<18> — https://assets2.hrc.org/files/assets/resources/2018-YouthReport-NoVid.pdf?_ga=2.27771068.1880459182.1550096788-1042517524.1532103907, Human Rights Campaign, 2018 LGBTQ Youth Report, When Schools Fail

<19> — https://assets2.hrc.org/files/assets/resources/2018-YouthReport-NoVid.pdf?_ga=2.27771068.1880459182.1550096788-1042517524.1532103907, Human Rights Campaign, 2018 LGBTQ Youth Report, Trans Youth Need Our Support

<20> — https://assets2.hrc.org/files/assets/resources/2018-YouthReport-NoVid.pdf?_ga=2.27771068.1880459182.1550096788-1042517524.1532103907, Human Rights Campaign, 2018 LGBTQ Youth Report, The Burden of Rejection

AFTERWORD

I hope you found my book informative. I hope you leave this book with a better understanding of yourself if you are transgender. If you are not transgender, I hope you have a better understanding of what being transgender is.

The information provided is gained from my life as a transgender woman. I also did much research for the nonprofit I was a part of and prior to starting my transition. I also did extensive research for this book on some of the topics I had less knowledge in. As I say in the book, information is power. Empower yourself to be the true you.

Please email me at Stephania@StephaniaKanitsch.com or message me on my website at https://www.spanninggenderbooks.com. I will try to answer questions within a few hours of receiving them.

Within the website, I will blog on topics of interest to the transgender and LGBTQ community. I also have Facebook set up where I post transgender and LGBTQ news of interest and importance.

APPENDIX ONE: DEFINITIONS AND ACRONYMS

It only serves to show what sort of person a man must be
who can't even get testimonials. No, no; if a man brings
references,
it proves nothing; but if he can't, it proves a great deal.
—Joseph Pulitzer

I f you are just coming out, information and references can become valuable. Prior to coming out, I tried to find as much information as I could. I read books, websites, support groups among many other sources. I am providing this chapter to give you information and references to allow you to have a successful and fulfilling transition. Please send me an email for any other references you may find. I will update a list online for those references not in this book.

Definitions Common to the Transgender Community

This list of definitions is not complete. The whole LGBTQ community adds unfamiliar words regularly. This transgender "dictionary" is far from inclusive. If you do not find a definition, please send me an email. I will add them to a list I maintain on my website.

Definition of Transgender Words:

Advocate: — A person acting on behalf of a marginalized group. They may provide education, promote social equity, and confront intolerance.

Agender: — This term encompasses many other genders. Agender is people who do not feel a gender or who feel their gender is neutral. Many agender people are outside the binary (transgender). Agender is a newer term. It is best as with anyone's gender to ask what gender they are or let them tell you.

AFAB and AMAB: — Acronyms meaning "assigned female/male at birth". (also, designated female/male at birth or female/male assigned at birth). No one gets to pick their assigned sex at birth. Transgender people prefer this term over biological male/female. There are other derogatory designations.

Affectional orientation: — Phrase used instead of sexual orientation.

Ally: — Cisgender and heterosexual people who advocate and support the transgender community. A person should not self-identify as an ally but show they are one through their actions.

Allyship: — Building relationships based on trust, consistency, and accountability with marginalized individuals and/or groups.

Androgyne/Androgynous/Androgyny: — A person with masculine and feminine physical traits. Centered on the gender spectrum.

Assigned sex at birth (ASAB): — Assumed sex at birth is what the sex a doctor claims you are. This term applies to intersex babies but applied to transgender people.

Bias incident: — An act intended to harm and/or harass a person based on their demographic background (s). For transgender people, this is because of their gender variance. For some, it also applies to other marginalized demographics that apply to them.

Bigender: — This refers to people who identify as two genders. A person can also identify as many genders (two or more genders). This does not include two-spirit. Two-spirit is a term used by native Americans and First Nations. See Two-spirit.

Binary: — Describes the genders female/male or woman/man. Binary genders are the only ones recognized by most of society as legitimate.

Body image: — How a person feels, acts and thinks about their body. Communities, families, cultures, media, and our perceptions form our attitudes about body image.

Bottom surgery: — Affirming surgery. Also known as Gender Confirmation Surgery (GCS).

Butch: — This is an identity that leans toward masculine. It does not limit this term to masculine lesbians. Associated with masculine queer/lesbian women, it may describe distinct gender identity and/or expression. This does not imply they identify as a female.

Cisnormativity: — A belief in only the gender binary male/female. This is an assumption being cisgender is right and transgender is wrong. This is a way to provide superiority for cisgender people over transgender people.

Cissexism/genderism: — A system of discrimination, harassment, and exclusion. This oppresses those whose gender and/or gender expression falls outside of cisnormativity. This also normalizes the belief that sex and gender are the same things.

Closeted: — A transgender — a person who knows they are transgender but has not come out yet. They may wait for their body characteristics to change to pass.

Cross-dressing (also cross-dressing): — The act of dressing and presenting as a different gender. Transvestite, a derogatory word, is an old term for a cross-dresser. Drag performers are cross-dressing performers. They take on stylized, exaggerated gender presentations. They do not identify as a cross-dresser. It does not tie cross-dressing to a person's gender. A person who has transitioned is not a cross-dresser. Please do not address them this way.

Demigender: — A partial gender identity. They may not feel a male or female. Demigender people are non-binary.

Designated sex at birth (DSAB): — The interpreted sex at birth. This is the same as assigned sex at birth. Ninety-eight percent of the population has sex characteristics identifiable as male or female. The other two percent may have ambiguous genitalia, such as intersex people. (These percentages are approximate)

Discrimination: — Unjust or prejudicial treatment of marginalized people. Examples are not allowing transgender people to use the proper bathroom.

Drag: — Exaggerated, theatrical, and/or performative gender presentation. Used most to refer to cross-dressing performers (drag queens and drag kings). Anyone of any gender can drag. This has nothing to do with a person's sex assigned at birth, gender identity, or sexual orientation.

Femme: — This is an identity that leans toward the feminine. It does not limit this term to feminine lesbians. It can imply a woman to a woman to "femme up", meaning to "woman" up. Although associated with feminine queer/lesbian women, it's used by many to describe distinct gender identity and/or expression. It does not imply that one also identifies as a female.

Fluid: — When applied to gender, a person whose gender moves around and is not static.

FTM (female to male): — See trans woman/trans man.

Vaginoplasty; Phalloplasty; Metoidioplasty: — Surgical realignment providing a transgender person's gender and primary sex characteristics to be more congruent. There is a small minority of the transgender community who opts for this surgery. There are many reasons for not opting, including cost. The following terms are inaccurate, offensive, or outdated: sex change operation, gender reassignment surgery, gender confirmation surgery, and sex reassignment surgery.

Gender binary: — The system where people view gender as only male or female. This system oppresses anyone who defies their sex assigned at birth.

Gender dysphoria: — Anxiety and/or discomfort of one's sex assigned at birth.

Gender-expansive: — A person who goes outside the boundary of the societal norm for gender. Anything beyond male and female. A synonym of gender variant.

Gender fluid: — A changing or "fluid" gender identity. See fluid.

Gender identity disorder/GID: — DSM-III and DSM-IV diagnosis identifying transgender and other gender non-conforming people. This term views transgender as a disorder. It may be offensive by some because of what it implies. The American Psychology Association replace this term with "gender dysphoria" in the DSM-5. Even though they replaced GID with gender dysphoria, the stigma remains.

Gender-neutral: — All-inclusive gender quality such as gender-neutral bathrooms.

Gender non-conforming (GNC): — Gender identity and expression are not aligned with societies norms.

Gender-normative: — When a person's gender identity and presentation align with societies norms. Opposite of gender non-conforming.

Gender outlaw: — Person who refuses to live by societies gender-normative attitude.

Gender presentation: — Outward gender expression of one's internal sense of gender. Synonym of gender expression.

Genderqueer: — A person does not identify in the gender binary. Genderqueer encompasses many other gender identities. Those who dislike labels may use this term. Binary and non-binary people may use this term. Genderqueer is neither transgender nor non-binary.

Gender role: — A role or behavior learned by a person as appropriate to their gender. Determined by the prevailing cultural norms.

Gender variant: — Gender variant is a behavior or gender expression by an individual not matching societal norms. When a person's gender identity and expression are no longer the gender binary. Synonym of gender-expansive.

Hermaphrodite: — Old word for intersex. This is a derogatory word.

Hormone replacement therapy (HRT): — The use of hormones to alter secondary sex characteristics. Not all transgender people take hormones.

Internalized oppression: — Members of a targeted group get socialized into believing oppressive beliefs they belong to. Many face the stereotypes and prejudices of the prejudices from an early age. It is easy to see how internalized oppression can take a person on.

Intersex: — Identifying those whose genitalia, chromosomes, and/or hormones do not match normal combinations. Their genitalia may be ambiguous. They may have androgen insensitivity syndrome (AIS) and many other differences. Doctors perform surgeries to match the ambiguous genitalia to a perceived gender. This surgery is mutilation of a baby who has no input in this decision. There are intersex people who identify as transgender. Intersex is about as common in society as redheads. (1.4 percent)

In the closet: — When a person has realized their identity but has not revealed it to anyone. Same as closeted.

MTF (male-to-female): — See trans woman/trans man.

Mis-gender: — Attributing a gender to someone who is not the gender. Using the wrong pronouns.

MOGAI: — An acronym standing for "marginalized orientations, gender alignments, and intersex." (LGBTQ replacement)

Mx.: — Gender-neutral salutation used in place of Ms., Mrs., or Mr.

Neutrois: — Non-binary gender identity. Neutrois falls under the genderqueer or transgender umbrellas.

Non-binary (Also non-binary): — Umbrella term for all genders other than female/male or woman/man. Not all non-binary people identify as trans and not all trans people identify as non-binary.

Omnigender: — Possessing all genders. Used to negate the belief of only two genders. Synonym for pangender and polygender.

Oppression: — When one group exploits another for its benefit.

Packing: — Wearing a penile prosthesis.

Pangender: — Many gender identities, expressions, and presentations. Synonym for omnigender and polygender.

Passing/blending/assimilating: — Ability of a transgender person to pass as their identified gender. For most transgender people, this would be their goal. For many, though, this is not reality.

Polygender: — Many gender identities, expressions, and presentations. Synonym for omnigender and pangender.

Pronouns: — Words to identify a person in the third person. In English and some other languages, it ties them to gender.

Queer: — General term for gender and sexual minorities who are not cisgender and/or heterosexual. They still use the word queer as a hateful slur. Some in the LGBTQ have reclaimed queer to identify themselves.

Questioning: — Exploring gender expression and identity. They also use this term as an identity for LGBTQ people.

Stealth: — To not identify as transgender in all or almost all social situations. The ability to pass as your gender is being stealth.

Stereotype: — A fixed assumption applied to all within a group. i.e. All gay people have HIV. All trans people are confused. This does not allow for individuality.

T: — Short for testosterone.

Third gender: — Anything outside of the gender binary.

Top surgery: — For transgender men, this is the removal of the breasts for more congruency in their gender. For transgender women, this is breast enhancement.

Trans: — Prefix or an adjective used as an abbreviation of transgender. Trans comes from the Latin word meaning "across from" or "on the other side of."

Transgender: — It signifies an array of identities under the trans umbrella.

Trans-misogyny: — Coined by author Julia Serano to name the intersections of transphobia and misogyny and how a person experiences them as oppression to transgender females.

Transphobia: — Systemic violence against trans people. Associated with attitudes such as fear, discomfort, distrust, or disdain. This word Like homophobia, xenophobia, misogyny, etc.

Trans woman/Trans man: — Trans woman describes someone assigned male at birth identifying as female. Trans man describes someone assigned female at birth identifying as male. This individual may or may not identify as trans. Many transgender individuals prefer a space between trans and woman/man. Others do not. Often it is respectable to use woman or man.

Sometimes trans women identify as male-to-female (also MTF, M2F, or trans feminine). Sometimes trans men identify as female-to-male (also FTM, F2M, or trans-masculine). Please ask before identifying someone. Use the term and pronouns preferred by the individual. MTF and FTM may be offensive to some.

Two-spirit: — An umbrella term indexing various indigenous gender identities in North America. Two-spirit may also apply to their affectional orientation.

Acronyms:

ASAB — Assigned sex at birth
AFAB — Assigned female at birth
AGAB — Assigned gender at birth
AIDS — Auto-Immune deficiency syndrome
AMAB — Assigned male at birth
ASAB — Assigned sex at birth
APA — American Psychological Association
DSD — Disorders of sexual development
FFS — Facial Feminine Surgery
FRC — Family Research Council
FTM — Female to male
GCS — Gender Confirmation Surgery
GLSEN — Once Gay, Lesbian & Straight Education Network
GNC — Gender non-conforming
HIV+ — Human immunodeficiency virus
HRT — Hormone replacement therapy
ISNA — Intersex Society of North America
LGBTQ — Lesbian, gay, bisexual, transgender, and queer or questioning
MTF — Male to female
NB — Non-binary
NCTE — National Center for Transgender Equality
PFLAG — Parents, Families, and Friends of Lesbians and Gays
SPLC — Southern Poverty Law Center
TDOR — Transgender Day of Remembrance
TLC — Transgender Law Center
USTS — United States Transgender Survey

APPENDIX TWO: TRANSGENDER SUPPORT ORGANIZATIONS

Family Equality Council — https://www.familyequality.org/
Family Equality Council - 475 Park Ave South, Suite 2100m - New York, NY 10016
Phone: 646-880-3005 - Fax: 646-880-3011
Family Equality Council's mission: Advance equality for LGBTQ families, and those wishing to form them. Accomplished through building community, changing hearts and minds, and driving policy change.

The GLBT National Help Center — https://www.glbthotline.org/
help@LGBThotline.org
LGBT National Help Center — 2261 Market Street, #296 — San Francisco, CA 94114
LGBT National Youth Talk line toll-free phone:
1-800-246-PRIDE (1-800-246-7743)
LGBT National Senior Talk line toll-free phone:
1-888-234-7243
Administrative phone: 415-355-0003
LGBT National Help Center, founded in 1996, is an organization providing vital peer-support, community connections, and resource information for people with questions about sexual orientation and/or gender identity.

Human Rights Campaign (HRC) — https://www.hrc.org/ — equalitycenter@hrc.org
Telephone: (800) 777-4723 — Fax: (202) 216-1596
Human Rights Campaign Foundation c/o Equality Center - 1640 Rhode Island Avenue NW - Washington, D.C. 20036
HRC's transgender resources — https://www.glaad.org/transgender/resources — (advocacy)
The Human Rights Campaign envisions an America where it ensures GLBT basic rights and can be open, honest and safe at home, at work, and in the community.

Parents, Family & Friends of Lesbians and Gays (PFLAG) — https://pflag.org/
https://pflag.org/contact-pflag (email)
PFLAG National Office — 1828 L Street, NW, Suite 660 — Washington, DC 20036
Main Phone: (202) 467-8180 — Fax: (202) 467-8194
PFLAG Our Trans Loved Ones (support for families of people who are trans) - https://pflag.org/ourtranslovedones

Gay & Lesbian Advocates & Defenders (GLAD) — https://www.glad.org/
gladlaw@glad.org
GLBTQ Legal Advocates & Defenders — 18 Tremont, Suite 950 — Boston, MA 02108
Phone: 617-426-1350 — Fax: 617-426-3594

Through strategic litigation, public policy advocacy, and education, GLAD works in New England and nationwide to create a society free of discrimination based on gender identity and expression, HIV status, and affectional orientation.

Lambda Legal Defense and Education Fund — https://www.lambdalegal.org/ Email Link

National Headquarters — 120 Wall Street, 19th Floor — New York, NY 10005-3919

Telephone 212-809-8585 — Fax 212-809-0055

Lambda Legal is the oldest and largest national legal civil rights organization. Their mission is to achieve full recognition for the civil rights of lesbians, gay men, bisexuals, transgender people. Also, everyone living with HIV through impact litigation, education, and public policy work.

Lambda Legal does not charge its clients for legal representation or advocacy. They receive no government funding. They depend on contributions from supporters around the country.

National Lesbian and Gay Law Association (NLGLA) — https://lgbtbar.org/

info@lgbtbar.org

1200 18th Street, NW, Suite 700 Washington, DC 20036

Phone: 202-637-7661

This is an organization of lawyers, judges, and other legal professionals, law students, activists. Also, affiliated lesbian, gay, bisexual, and transgender legal organizations. The NLGLA promotes justice through the legal profession for the LGBTQ+ community.

Transgender Law Center (TLC) — https://transgenderlawcenter.org/

info@transgenderlawcenter.org

Transgender Law Center — PO Box 70976 — Oakland, CA 94612-0976

Phone: 510-587-9696 — Collect line for inmates & detainees: 510-380-8229

Fax: 510-587-9699 — Legal Help: 415-865-0176

TLC changes law, policy, and attitudes so that all people can live in a safe and authentic atmosphere. Also free from discrimination regardless of their gender identity or expression.

Advocates for Informed Choice (AIC) — https://aiclegal.WordPress.com/

info@aiclegal.org

Advocates for Informed Choice — P.O. Box 676 — Cotati, CA 94931

Phone: 707-793-1190

AIC uses innovative legal strategies to advocate for the civil rights of children born with variations of reproductive or sexual anatomy.

APPENDIX THREE: TRANSGENDER SUPPORT FOR PROFESSIONALS

Gay, Lesbian & Straight Educators Network (GLSEN) — https://www.glsen.org/
info@glsen.org
GLSEN, Inc. — 110 William Street, 30th Floor — New York, NY 10038
Phone: 212-727-0135
GLSEN creates safe schools for all, regardless of sexual orientation and gender identity/expression. They dedication provides a work environment and designing programs and resources that are inclusive and celebratory of diversity, and sensitive to the role of power and privilege in society.

Gay and Lesbian Medical Association (GLMA) — http://www.glma.org/
info@glma.org
GLMA — 1133 19th Street, NW, Suite 302 — Washington, DC 20036
Phone: 202-600-8037 — Fax: 202-478-1500
The GLMA's mission is to ensure equality in healthcare for LGBT individuals and healthcare professionals. They achieve their goals by using the health and medical expertise of its members. They provide professional education, public policy work, patient education, and referrals, and promote research.

National Gay and Lesbian Chamber of Commerce (NGLCC) — https://www.nglcc.org
info@nglcc.org
NGLCC — 1331 F Street | Suite 900 — Washington, D.C. 20004
Phone: 202-234-9181 — Fax: 202-234-9185
NGLCC Global is dedicated to advancing the economic empowerment of LGBTI people everywhere.

APPENDIX FOUR: WORKPLACE SUPPORT FOR THE TRANSGENDER INDIVIDUAL

Out and Equal Workplace Advocates — http://outandequal.org/
hello@outandequal.org
Out and Equal — 155 Sansome St, Ste 450 — San Francisco, California 94104
Phone: 415-694-6500
Their mission is to "educate and empower organizations, human resource professionals, Employee Resource Groups (ERGs) and individual employees through programs and services resulting in equal policies, opportunities, practices, and benefits in the workplace regardless of sexual orientation, gender identity, expression, or characteristics,".

APPENDIX FIVE: SUPPORT FOR THE TRANSGENDER VETERAN

American Veterans for Equal Rights (AVER) — http://aver.us/
info@aver.us
AVER, Inc. — PMB 416 — 15127 Main Street E, Ste 104 — Sumner, WA 98390
Phone: 718-849-5665
They are LGBT-founded veterans' advocacy and service organization. They dedicate their work to the equal and fair treatment of all service members and veterans. Also honoring the service and sacrifices of all service members and veterans."

OutServe-SLDN — https://www.OutServe-SLDN.org/
admin@outserve-sldn.org
OutServe-SLDN — 1133 19th St. NW — Washington DC 20036
Phone: 800-538-7418
Educate the community, provide legal services, advocate for authentic transgender service, provide developmental opportunities, support members and local chapters, communicate in an efficient manner and work towards equality for all.

APPENDIX SIX: SUPPORT FOR THE TRANSGENDER ELDERLY

Services & Advocacy for Gay, Lesbian, Bisexual & Transgender Elders (SAGE) — https://sagenyc.org/nyc/
SAGE — 305 Seventh Ave, 15th Floor — New York, NY 10001
Phone: 212-741-2247 — Fax: 212-366-1947
SAGE offers innovative services and programs to LGBT older people throughout New York City and nationwide through our affiliate network, SAGENet. From arts and culture to health and wellness, employment help, and much more.

APPENDIX SEVEN: RESOURCES FOR THE TRANSGENDER INDIVIDUAL IN CRISIS

The Trevor Project — https://www.thetrevorproject.org/
info@thetrevorproject.org
The Trevor Project — PO Box 69232 — West Hollywood, CA 90069
24/7/365 Lifeline — 866-4-U-TREVOR (866-488-7386)
TrevorChat, https://www.thetrevorproject.org/get-help-now/#sm.001608re7jw8fqi10w92gbc8temt7, their online instant messaging option
TrevorText, https://www.thetrevorproject.org/get-help-now/#sm.001608re7jw8fqi10w92gbc8temt7a, text-based support option
The Trevor Project's mission is to end suicide among gay, lesbian, bisexual, transgender, queer & questioning young people. The organization works to fulfill this mission through four strategies:
• Provide crisis counseling to LGBTQ young people thinking of suicide.
• Offer resources, supportive counseling, and a sense of community to LGBTQ young people to reduce the risk they become suicidal.
• Educate young people and adults who interact with young people on LGBTQ-competent suicide prevention, risk detection and response.
• Advocate for laws and policies that will reduce suicide among LGBTQ young people.

The National Suicide Prevention Lifeline — https://suicidepreventionlifeline.org/
24/7/365 Lifeline: 800-273-TALK (8255) — Espanol — 888-628-9454 — Deaf and Hard of Hearing: 800-799-4889
The National Suicide Prevention Lifeline is a national network of local crisis centers that provides free and confidential emotional support to people in a suicidal crisis or emotional distress 24 hours a day, 7 days a week. They commit to improving crisis services and advancing suicide prevention by empowering individuals, advancing professional best practices, and building awareness.

Trans Lifeline — https://www.translifeline.org/ — contact@translifeline.org
Trans Lifeline — 101 Broadway #311 — Oakland, CA 94607
Lifeline USA: 877-565-8860 — Canada: 877-330-6366
Office: 510-771-1417
Trans Lifeline is a national trans-led organization dedicated to improving the quality of trans lives by responding to the critical needs of our community with direct service, material support, advocacy, and education. Our vision is to fight the epidemic of trans suicide and improve life-outcomes of trans people by facilitating justice-oriented, collective community aid. The Trevor Project —

https://www.thetrevorproject.org/, info@thetrevorproject.org, **The Trevor Project —** PO Box 69232 — West Hollywood, CA 90069

APPENDIX EIGHT: TRANSGENDER ADVOCACY ORGANIZATIONS

National Center for Transgender Equality (NCTE) (advocacy) —
https://transequality.org/ — ncte@transequality.org
NCTE — 1133 19th St NW — Suite 302 — Washington D. C. 20036
Phone: 202-642-4542
The National Center for Transgender Equality advocates changing policies and
society to increase understanding and acceptance of transgender people. In the
nation's capital and throughout the country, NCTE works to replace disrespect,
discrimination, and violence with empathy, opportunity, and justice.

Freedom for All Americans (policy and legislative advocacy) —
https://www.freedomforallamericans.org/
Freedom for All Americans — 1629 K St NW — Suite 300 — Washington, DC 20006
Phone: 202-601-0187
This is a bipartisan campaign to secure full non-discrimination protections for
LGBTQ people nationwide. Their work brings together Republicans and Democrats,
businesses large and small, people of faith, and allies from all levels of society to
make the case for comprehensive non-discrimination protections for fair treatment
of all.

COLAGE Kids of Trans Community (support for kids of trans parents) —
https://www.colage.org/kot/
colage@colage.org
COLAGE — 3815 S. Othello Street, Suite 100, #310, — Seattle, WA 98118
Phone: 828-782-1938
COLAGE unites people with lesbian, gay, bisexual, transgender, and/or queer parents
and caregivers into a network of peers. They provide support to nurture and empower
all to be skilled, self-confident and leaders in our collective communities.

The Task Force — http://www.thetaskforce.org/ — thetaskforce@thetaskforce.org
The Task Force — 1325 Massachusetts Ave. NW — Suite 600 — Washington, DC
20005
Phone: 202-393-5177 — Fax: 202-393-2241
Trans/gender non-conforming justice project — thetaskforce@thetaskforce.org —
(advocacy)
The National LGBTQ Task Force advances full freedom, justice, and equality for LGBTQ
people.
They are building a future where everyone is free to be themselves in every aspect of
their lives. Today, millions of LGBTQ people face barriers in every part of their lives: in

housing, employment, healthcare, retirement, and basic human rights. These barriers must go. Therefore, the Task Force is training and mobilizing millions of activists across our nation.

American Civil Liberties Union (ACLU) (legal services) — https://www.aclu.org/
ACLU — 125 Broad Street, 18th Floor — New York NY 10004
Phone: 212-549-2500
The ACLU is a nonprofit organization whose mission is "to defend and preserve the individual rights and liberties guaranteed to every person by the Constitution and laws of the United States."

National Center for Lesbian Rights - Transgender Law (legal services) — http://www.nclrights.org/our-work/transgender-law/transgender-youth/
Info@NCLRights.org
870 Market Street, Suite 370 — San Francisco, CA 94102
Legal Help Line—1.800.528.6257 or 415-392-6257 — Fax: 415-392-8442
NCLR is a national legal organization committed to advancing the civil and human rights of lesbian, gay, bisexual, and transgender people and their families. They do this through litigation, legislation, policy, and public education. Their community and public education broadens public support for LGBT equality.

TransJustice at the Audre Lorde Project (AIP)(advocacy) — https://alp.org/
jessica@alp.org
ALP — 147 West 24th Street, 3rd Floor — New York, NY 10011-1911
Phone: 212-463-0342 · Fax: 212-463-0344
ALP is a Lesbian, Gay, Bisexual, Two Spirit, Trans and Gender Non-Conforming People of Color center for community organizing, focusing on the New York City area. Through mobilization, education, and capacity-building, they work for community wellness and progressive social and economic justice. Committed to struggling across differences, they seek to reflect, represent, and serve our various communities.

APPENDIX NINE: GENERAL TRANSGENDER INFORMATION WEBSITES

Trans Students Educational Resource (TSER) — http://transstudent.org/
tser@transstudent.org
No address or phone number
TSER is a youth-led organization dedicated to transforming the educational environment for trans and gender non-conforming students. They accomplish this through advocacy and empowerment. They also focus on creating a trans-friendly education system. Their mission is to educate the public and teach trans activists on how to be effective organizers. They believe justice for trans and gender non-conforming youth is contingent on an intersectional framework of activism. Ending oppression is a long-term process achievable through collaborative action.

El/La Para TransLatinas — http://ellaparatranslatinas.yolasite.com/
essie@ellaparatranslatinas.org
El/La Para TransLatinas — 2940 16th St Suite 319 — San Francisco, CA 94103
Phone: 415-864-7278
Luchamos por los derechos de las translatinas. Buscamos crear un mundo en el cual nosotras las translatinas sentimos que merecemos protegernos, amarnos y desarrollar nuestras personas. Sobre esta base, nos apoyamos en protegernos de la violencia, el abuso y la enfermedad.

Sylvia Rivera Law Project — https://srlp.org/ — info@srlp.org
SRLP — 147 W 24th St, 5th Floor — New York, NY 10011
Phone: 212-337-8550 — Fax: 212-337-1972
The SRLP works to guarantee all people are free to self-determine their gender identity and expression. This is regardless of income or race, and without facing harassment, discrimination, or violence. SRLP is a collective organization founded on the understanding that gender self-determination is intertwined with racial, social and economic justice. They seek to increase the political voice and visibility of low-income people and people of color who are transgender, intersex, or gender non-conforming. SRLP works to improve access to respectful and affirming social, health, and legal services for our communities. They believe that to create meaningful political participation and leadership, we must have access to basic means of survival and safety from violence.

Transcending Boundaries Conference — https://www.transcendingboundaries.org/
inf@transcendingboundaries.org
Transcending Boundaries, Inc. — PO Box 30171 — Springfield, MA 01103
No Phone

Transcending Boundaries, Inc. is a 501 (c)(3) nonprofit organization which provides education, activism, and support for persons whose sexuality, gender, sex, or relationship style do not fit within conventional categories. The organization serves our ever-evolving communities, including bisexual, pansexual, fluid, queer, transgender, transsexual, genderqueer, intersex, asexual, polyamorous, and kinky persons, and allies and those who prefer not to use labels. Our work includes an annual conference, community outreach, and educational resources.

Transgender Archive — https://www.digitaltransgenderarchive.net/
https://www.digitaltransgenderarchive.net/contact email link
No address
No phone
The purpose of the Digital Transgender Archive (DTA) is to increase the accessibility of transgender history by providing an online hub for digitized historical materials, born-digital materials, and information on archival holdings worldwide. Based in Worcester, Massachusetts at the College of the Holy Cross, the DTA is an international collaboration among over fifty colleges, universities, nonprofit organizations, public libraries, and private collections. By digitally localizing a wide range of trans-related materials, the DTA expands access to trans history for academics and independent researchers alike to foster education and dialog concerning trans history.

Transgender Foundation of America — http://www.tfahouston.com/
info@tgctr.org
Transgender Foundation of America — PO Box 542287 — Houston, TX 77254
No phone number
TFA provides homeless services and removes barriers to mental health support through free group therapy, counseling, and vetted referrals. TFA supports community development through providing free meeting space to groups and by hosting regular events that strengthen ties within the GLBT community.

Transsexual and Transgender Roadmap — https://www.transgendermap.com/
Andrea James — 5419 Hollywood Blvd. # C-142 — Los Angeles, CA 90027
Transsexual and Transgender Roadmap is a site offering a large amount of information on figuring out you are transgender and transitioning. The website provides resources and general information.

APPENDIX TEN: VARIOUS OTHER INFORMATION WEBSITES

Lynn Conway — http://www.lynnconway.com
Lynn Conway is a transgender professor. She transitioned in 1968, a time when transgender people stayed hidden because of the hate and stigma. They outed her in 1999 through previous work she had accomplished prior to her transition. Lynn's research, along with Carver Mead discovered VLSI Technology used for miniaturizing computers. She founded other technologies along with her storied career. Lynn's website has information on her transition, her work, and her life. There is also information on being transgender and transitioning. Lynn is one of many transgender pioneers that helped us to be who we are today.

Gender Psychology — http://www.genderpsychology.org
madeline@genderpsychology.org
Madeline is a psychology professor who is also transgender (bigender). She has her story on her site about her struggles in finding herself. She has put together some nice material from her perspective as a psychology professor and being transgender. There are many wonderful links on her website.

APPENDIX ELEVEN: ORGANIZATIONS AGAINST REPARATIVE THERAPY

American Academy of Child and Adolescent Psychiatry, Policy Statement:
The American Academy of Child and Adolescent Psychiatry finds no evidence to support the application of any "therapeutic intervention" operating under the premise that a specific sexual orientation, gender identity, and/or gender expression is pathological. Based on the scientific evidence, the AACAP asserts that such "conversion therapies" (or other interventions imposed intending to promote sexual orientation and/or gender as a preferred outcome) lack scientific credibility and clinical utility. There is evidence that such interventions are harmful. As a result, "conversion therapies" should not be part of any behavioral health treatment of children and adolescents

American Academy of Family Physicians,
American Academy of Nursing,
American Association of Sexuality Educators, Counselors, and Therapists,
American Counseling Association,
American Medical Association,
American Medical Student Association,
American Psychoanalytic Association,
The Association of LGBTQ Psychiatrists,
Association of Lesbian, Gay, Bisexual, Transgender Issues in Counseling,
Clinical Social Work Association,
Gay and Lesbian Medical Association,
The Association of Lesbian, Gay, Bisexual, Transgender Addiction Professionals, and their Allies, &
World Professional Association for Transgender Health,
Joint Statement (Draft):
The signatories of this statement share a commitment to protecting the public from the risks and harms of conversion therapy and to ensuring full access to the benefits of ethical, affirmative healthcare for sexual and gender minorities. Given the fact that same-sex desire and behavior and gender variant identity and expression are not mental disorders, and given the lack of evidence showing that conversion therapy can effectively change sexual orientation or gender identity, and given the strong indications that such change efforts can increase stigma and cause other harms to patients and their families, we urge all healthcare professionals to commit themselves to ensure that: [...]

American Academy of Pediatrics, Policy Statement:

In contrast, "conversion" or "reparative" treatment models are used to prevent children and adolescents from identifying as transgender or to dissuade them from exhibiting gender diverse expressions. [...] Reparative approaches have been proven to be not only unsuccessful but also deleterious and are considered outside the mainstream of traditional medical practice.

American Group Psychotherapy Association,
American Mental Health Counselors Association,
Gay and Lesbian Medical Association,
National Association for Children's Behavioral Health,
National Association of School Psychologists, &
National Coalition for Mental Health Recovery,
To Whom It May Concern:
There is virtually no credible evidence that any type of psychotherapy can change a person's sexual orientation, gender identity or expression, and, in fact, conversion efforts pose critical health risks to lesbian, gay, bisexual, and transgender people, including depression, shame, decreased self-esteem, social withdrawal, substance abuse, risky behavior, and suicidality

---

American Medical Association, Policy H-160.991:
Our AMA: [...] (c) opposes, the use of "reparative" or "conversion" therapy for sexual orientation or gender identity.

American Psychiatric Association, Approved resource document*:
Expert consensus regarding the treatment of adults has been arrived at after many years of clinical experience. Attempts to engage individuals in psychotherapy to change their gender identity or expression are currently not considered fruitful by the mental health professionals with the most experience working in this area and legal bans of therapies aimed at changing sexual orientation have recently been extended to therapies aimed at changing gender identity or expression in a number of U.S. states and Canadian provinces. Currently, psychotherapeutic involvement with adults with GD is primarily used to assist in clarifying their desire for, and commitment to, changes in gender expression and/or somatic treatments to minimize discordance with their experienced gender, and to ensure that they are aware of and have considered alternatives.
*This document only explicitly opposes conversion or reparative therapy for adults.

American Psychoanalytic Association, Position Statement:
Psychoanalytic technique does not encompass purposeful attempts to "convert," "repair," change or shift an individual's sexual orientation, gender identity or gender expression. Such directed efforts are against fundamental principles of psychoanalytic treatment and often result in substantial psychological pain by reinforcing damaging internalized attitudes.

American Psychological Association &
National Association of School Psychologists,
Resolution:
BE IT FURTHER RESOLVED that the American Psychological Association and the National Association of School Psychologists support affirmative interventions with transgender and gender diverse children and adolescents that encourage self-exploration and self-acceptance rather than trying to shift gender identity and gender expression in any specific direction;

American School Counselor Association, Position statement:
It is not the school counselor's role to change a student's sexual orientation or gender identity. School counselors recognize the profound harm intrinsic to therapies alleging to change an individual's sexual orientation or gender identity [...] and advocate to protect LGBTQ students from this harm.

Association of Christian Counselors,
British Association for Counselling and Psychotherapy,
British Association of Behavioral and Cognitive Psychotherapies,
British Psychoanalytic Council,
British Psychological Society,
College of Sex and Relationship Therapists,
GLADD (The Association of LGBT Doctors and Dentists),
National Counselling Society,
NHS England,
NHS Scotland,
Pink Therapy,
Royal College of General Practitioners, &
UK Council for Psychotherapy,
Memorandum of Understanding:
For this document 'conversion therapy' is an umbrella term for a therapeutic approach, or any model or individual viewpoint that shows an assumption that any sexual orientation or gender identity is inherently preferable to any other, and which attempts to bring about a change of sexual orientation or gender identity or seeks to suppress an individual's expression of sexual orientation or gender identity on that basis. [...] Signatory organizations agree that the practice of conversion therapy, whether in relation to sexual orientation or gender identity, is unethical and potentially harmful.

Australian and New Zealand Professional Association for Transgender Health,
Standards of Care:
In the past, psychological practices attempting to change a person's gender identity to be more aligned with their sex assigned at birth were used. Such practices,

typically known as conversion or reparative therapies, lack efficacy, are considered unethical and may cause lasting damage to a child or adolescent's social and emotional health and well-being.

Canadian Association of Social Workers &
Canadian Association for Social Work Education,
Joint Statement:
Any professional's attempt to alter the gender identity or expression of a young person to align with social norms is considered unethical and an abuse of power and authority. Specifically, social workers should reject any attempt to prevent a child from growing up to be transgender, transsexual, two-spirit, gay, lesbian, bisexual or queer.

Canadian Professional Association for Transgender Health, Submission in support of Bill 77:
Clearly, conversion "therapy" and clinical or "therapeutic" interventions that counsel parents to make their affection, love, and support conditional on restricting a child's gender identity or expression, or that instill shame on children and youth for their gender identity or gender expression are inconsistent with an overwhelming consensus of major mental health organizations have no place in professional practice.

Canadian Psychiatric Association,
Policy statement:
The CPA opposes the use of reparative or conversion therapy, given that such therapy assumes that LGBTQ identities indicate a mental disorder and (or) the assumption that the person could and should change their sexual orientation and (or) their gender identity and gender expression.

College of Registered Psychotherapists of Ontario,
Practice Standards:
Seeking to change or direct a person's sexual orientation or gender identity is not 'therapy', are not supported by the profession and do not respect the diversity and dignity of all persons.

International Federation of Social Workers, Statement of Principles:
Social workers must not allow their knowledge and skills to be used for inhumane purposes, such as [...] conversion therapy [...].

Ordre professionel des sexologues du Québec (Professional order of sexologists of Quebec), Public statement (translated):
The Professional order of sexologists of Quebec wishes to inform individuals who might want to receive [conversion or reparative therapy] for themselves or their child [...] that they are prohibited by many regions of the world and by most professional associations in psychology, psychiatry, and medicine as well as

professional orders including the Professional order of sexologists of Quebec, as the present statement evidence.

National Association of Social Workers' National Committee on LGBT Issues,

Position Statement:

The term sexual orientation change efforts (or SOCE) include any practice seeking to change a person's sexual orientation, including, but not limited to, efforts to change behaviors, gender identity, or gender expressions, or to reduce or eliminate sexual or romantic attractions or feelings toward a person of the same gender.

The practice of SOCE violates the very tenets of the social work profession as outlined in the NASW Code of Ethics. [...] The National Committee on LGBT Issues asserts that conversion therapy or SOCE is an infringement of the guiding principles inherent to social worker ethics and values; a position affirmed by the NASW policy statement on "Lesbian, Gay, and Bisexual Issues" (NASW 2014).

NHS England,

Service Specifications:

Providers will not deliver, promote or refer individuals to any form of conversion therapy. The practice of conversion therapy is unethical and potentially harmful.

*This document only explicitly opposes conversion or reparative therapy for adults. For a statement including youth, see NHS England's endorsement of the Memorandum of Understanding.

Royal College of Psychiatrists,

Position Statement:

The term 'conversion therapy' has also been used to describe treatments for transgender people that aim to suppress or divert their gender identity — i.e. to make them cisgender — that is exclusively identified with the sex assigned to them at birth. Conversion therapies may draw from treatment principles established for other purposes, for example, psychoanalytic or behavior therapy. They may include barriers to gender-affirming medical and psychological treatments. There is no scientific support for use of treatments in such a way and such applications are widely regarded as unacceptable.

Society for Adolescent Health and Medicine,

Position paper:

Reparative "therapy," which attempts to change one's sexual orientation or gender identity, is inherently coercive and inconsistent with current standards of medical care.

Substance Abuse and Mental Health Services Administration,

Consensus Statement:

Interventions aimed at a fixed outcome, such as gender conformity or heterosexual orientation, including those aimed at changing gender identity, gender expression, and sexual orientation are coercive, can be harmful, and should not be part of behavioral health treatment. Directing the child to be conforming to any gender expression or sexual orientation or directing the parents to place pressure for specific gender expressions, gender identities, and sexual orientations are inappropriate and reinforce harmful gender and sexual orientation stereotypes.

It is clinically inappropriate for behavioral health professionals to have a prescriptive goal related to gender identity, gender expression, or sexual orientation for the ultimate developmental outcome of a child's or adolescent's gender identity or gender expression.

World Professional Association in Transgender Health, Standards of Care:
Treatment aimed at trying to change a person's gender identity and expression to become more congruent with sex assigned at birth has been attempted in the past without success [...], particularly in the long-term [...]. Such treatment is no longer considered ethical.

APPENDIX TWELVE: TRANSGENDER PRONUNCIATIONS IN OTHER PARTS OF THE WORLD

Burma — Acault
Cook Islands — Akava'ine
Central Asia — Bacchá
Philippines — Bakla
Eunuch
India — Evening people
Tonga — Fakaleiti
Samoa — Fa'afafine
Neapolitan — Femminiello
ancient Rome — Galli
Thailand — Kathoey
Arabia — Khanith
Egypt — Khawal
Turkey — Köçek
Hawaii — Mahuwahine
Burma — Meinmasha
Nepal — Meti
Malaysia — Maknyah
the Langi in Uganda — Mudoko dako
Arabia — Mukhannathun
Mexico — Muxe
Japan — Newhalf ("ニューハーフ")
China — Transgender
Singapore — Transgender people
Thailand — Tom-Dee identity
Balkan — Sworn virgin
Maori — Takatāpui
Brazil — Travesti
North America (indigenous) — Two-Spirit/"Berdache"
Indonesia — Waria

APPENDIX THIRTEEN: DIFFERENT HORMONES AND THEIR USUAL DOSING

Table of medications taken by transgender people to aid in transition – Female to Male

Medication	Usual dosing	Route of entry
Testosterone		
Cypionate Testosterone enanthate	50-200 mg/wk 100-200 mg/10-14 days	Subcutaneous (shot) intramuscular
Testopel	75 mg/pellet	Transdermal
Testosterone gel (1%)	2.5-10 g/day	Gel
Testosterone patch	2.5-7.5 mg/day	patch

Table of medications taken by transgender people to aid in transition – Male to Female

Medication	Usual dosing	Route of entry
Estradiol		
Estradiol	2-4 mg/day	Oral
Estradiol valerate	5-30 mg/2 weeks	Parental (subcutaneous, intramuscular
Estradiol	0.1-0.4 mg/twice weekly	Trandermal
Anti-androgen		
Progesterone	20-60 mg PO/daily	Oral
Medroxyprogesterone acetate	150 mg/every 3 months	Intramuscular
GnRH agonist (leuprolide)	3.75-7.5 mg/monthly	Intramuscular
Histrelin	50 mg/12 months	Implanted
Spironlactone	100-200 mg PO/daily	Oral
Finasteride	1 mg PO/daily	Oral

SPECIAL THANKS TO

I would like to give special thanks to the following people, who helped me to put this project together. I am indebted to those who helped me with this dream.

Robert Ruff and Megan Klaeger Ruff – You two supplied the means to have a professional book cover published. Robert and Megan are both wonderful advocates for the LGBTQ community and have given of themselves for betterment. I am proud to call them friends.

Susan (you know who you are) – Thank you for reading my book to help in the editing of the contents. You gave a lot of input to ensure the information was as complete as possible.

Barb Warden – Thank you for reading, editing and correcting punctuation and grammar for me. My first through on any writing is atrocious. I am getting better on the third, fourth, and fifth read through.

Chris Alvarenga – Thanks to Chris for reading and providing me with errors she found. Your input was priceless.

Cari Foote – Many thanks for Cari's input, read, corrections, and updates.

Cari, Chris, and Barb all inspired me to continue writing after I left the nonprofit helped me make it through some tough times. I am very appreciative to you all.

W

Y

ABOUT THE AUTHOR

Stephania M. Kanitsch was a metrologist at the Palo Verde Nuclear Power Station. She now spends her time authoring books and advocating for the transgender community when she can. Stephania was a board member and vice president of a nonprofit. She found that her passion for the transgender and LGBTQ community came out in the seminars she wrote while at the nonprofit. Her home is in the Central Texas Hill Country.